God's Little Aphorisms

God's Little Aphorisms

✦

One-Liners from The Source

by Beth Green

iUniverse, Inc.
New York Lincoln Shanghai

God's Little Aphorisms
One-Liners from The Source

Copyright © 2005 by Beth Green

iUniverse books may be ordered through booksellers or by contacting:

iUniverse
2021 Pine Lake Road, Suite 100
Lincoln, NE 68512
www.iuniverse.com
1-800-Authors (1-800-288-4677)

Cover design by Cara Carlson.
Interior graphic by Cara Carlson.
The interior graphic is The Stream logo and is used with permission. Beth Green is the spiritual director of The Stream, a nonprofit educational corporation, www.thestream.org.

ISBN: 0-595-34522-0

Printed in the United States of America

Contents

Introduction

What are God's little aphorisms? First, for those not familiar with the word, an aphorism is a zinger, a terse saying that catches our attention and reveals some truth, such as "Haste makes waste." And, second, what is God? To me, God is the source of the universe, the totality, the one who sees the big picture.

So *God's Little Aphorisms* is a collection of short sayings that come from a consciousness greater than my own. These one-liners make me laugh, think and change. They're zingers from the source. And you can enjoy and use them, whether you believe in "God" or not!

God's little aphorisms have come to me through the inner voice, the voice in my head that is smarter than I am. Some people call it channeling. Here's the way it can happen. Say I'm struggling with some crisis, feeling lost and confused. My mind is going in circles, and I see no way out. Suddenly through the inner voice, I "hear" a great one-liner that stops me in my tracks. The message is clear and compelling. It makes me laugh at myself and gives me a new perspective, a different way to feel or behave. I say it's from God, because the voice in my head is always smarter than I am. It sure isn't me!

I started receiving these zingers in 1980, when I had a spiritual/psychic awakening and developed the inner voice and other forms of intuitive knowing. Since that time, intuition has guided my counseling, healing and spiritual teaching, and it has guided my life.

Over these many years, God has used my inner voice to shower me with an abundance of aphorisms. Although I've shared these one-liners with friends and clients, I have never written them down. Some have stuck in my mind, and some have been forgotten. Recently people have been asking me to write them out and to make them available to them and others. And so I have. And I'm still writing—still remembering, and still receiving more.

Out of the many aphorisms I've received, God has chosen 52 to include in this first volume. Many of these focus on the nature of God, oneness, judgment and compassion. Because these topics are covered so frequently in this first volume, we can be sure they are foundations for our spiritual growth and wellbeing. Other topics are covered as well, and additional ones will be found in future volumes.

The format of the book is this: First I quote the aphorism itself, and then I offer a few paragraphs describing its application. Sometimes I've also included a little story about the circumstances under which I got the message. I hope you find these stories fun and clarifying.

The aphorisms may be God's, but the commentaries are mine, meaning you may give these sayings any interpretation you want. In fact, please use this volume in any way that suits you. Some people will want to read it through; others will want to dip randomly; and since there are 52, still others will want to take one a week as a spiritual focus. It might be fun to study an aphorism and then see how many times you can apply it in your life that day, that week or even over time.

Even though these aphorisms have been coming to me for well over twenty years, they have never gotten old or outlived their usefulness. They have really helped me, and I hope they'll help you, too. If they do, look forward to more in the future. I've got lots to share. Thanks.

God's Little Aphorisms

1

"If you had been meant to know everything, I wouldn't have had to create other people."

I have always tended to put a lot of pressure on myself, and when I became an intuitive counselor and spiritual teacher, I was even more under the gun. After all, wasn't I a representative of God? Wasn't I an intuitive? Wasn't I supposed to know everything?

Fortunately, God stopped me in my tracks on this one. One day, I was facilitating a women's group and during that group, a client hit upon a great idea that had not occurred to me. She made a connection I hadn't. Naturally, I immediately felt shame. How come this client had seen the answer while I, the great leader, was still in the dark?

That's when God told me, "If you had been meant to know everything, Beth, I wouldn't have had to create other people." From that moment, I started laughing at my foolishness, and I haven't stopped laughing since.

What more perfect way to start this book than to admit to you that I don't know everything. In fact, I'm not supposed to know everything, and neither are you.

Where did we get the idea that we are supposed to know everything, anyway? Is it a way to feel powerful, in control and independent?

None of us is independent. We rely on one another to raise and transport the food that feeds us, build the homes that shelter us, manufacture the cars that transport us, and create the music that inspires us. Not to speak of how much we rely on one another for love and companionship. But ironically, while we feel that it's okay to depend on others for food, homes, cars and music, many of us feel we're not supposed to be dependent on one another for wisdom! In fact many of us live in fear that someone will discover that we don't know something we think they think we should know.

Maybe when we were kids, we were shamed for not knowing something at home. Or maybe we were ridiculed for not knowing something in school. Whatever the cause, though, many of us are afraid that we'll be mocked if we're caught without "the answer." Guided by this aphorism, we have a new perspective. "If I had meant you to know everything, I wouldn't have had to create other people" tells us that, since God obviously created other people, we're not *supposed* to know everything. In fact, the opposite is the case. We're actually supposed to rely on one another. Why? Because by making us mentally interdependent, the universe is compelling us to find a way to work together, to break out of our self-centered individualism, to learn the spiritual truth that we are one.

So no matter what the field, be it our business, the raising of our children, or even our spiritual development, it is neither necessary nor preferable to know everything. We're *supposed* to be only part of the puzzle. We're *supposed* to need one another's perceptions and wisdom. We're supposed to remember we are one.

Not knowing makes us not less, but more—more open to one another, more able to receive from one another, and more able to give to one another the gift of appreciation for each other's wisdom. So thanks for knowing what I don't, and feel free to share the wisdom I've been given.

2

"God is not part of your mission; you are part of my plan."

When I first started hearing the inner voice, I felt very important, as though I had been chosen for some high-level mission. This was both thrilling and scary.

So you can imagine that I experienced a combination of embarrassment and relief when God told me that she was not part of my mission; I was part of her plan.

I realize now, of course, that my earlier state of mind was just a normal human reaction to suddenly having a "special" relationship with God. Out of the blue, I had become able to channel higher consciousness and deliver definitive commentary on every- and anything. Wow, how important and powerful was I! This behavior was just an example of the insecure little me trying to impress myself and you, so as to gain attention and admiration from others, like a kid who says, "Look at me. Look at me."

But using God as part of my mission also reflected a world view that was upside down. It's the world view that probably most of us share, which is that I, the individual, am the center of the universe, and every-thing revolves around me. Now that's funny.

In my current belief system, God represents the whole, the totality. So if God were part of *my* mission, then God, the whole, would be part of me, the part; rather than me, the part, being part of God, the whole. Now does that make sense?

It's part of our culture to see the individual as the center of the universe. So it was very natural for me to automatically think that God existed to help me achieve my mission—as though *I* were the one to determine what's meant to be, and it were God's job to assist me in the accomplish-ment of it.

I'm not the only one who thinks this way. Don't you ever do it? Don't we all have a tendency to pray to God to help us achieve some goal we've decided is best for us and everyone else? Don't we ask God to help us "save" somebody we think needs saving, or to help us get some job, snag a great husband or even kill the people we've decided are bad?

"What's wrong with that?" you ask with a grin. "Are you telling me that I'm *not* the center of the universe and that God is *not* going to mold to my wishes and desires?"

In a way, when I look at the planet as a whole, I can see myself as an ant in a colony—a very special ant, of course, but an ant nonetheless. And there's relief in that. It means that I have buddies to help me move that dirt and to meet my needs and those of everyone else. And it means that the whole universe is not relying on my intelligence. Phew!

So while it is deflating to realize that I am part of a bigger whole, a part of God's plan, I can now actually relax into the realization that I am not responsible for the destiny of the universe; God is.

I might not be sure that God has a plan, and if she does, I might not like it, but thank heavens the salvation of the planet doesn't rest on my shoulders, because I really don't have all the answers. If I ever thought I did, my years on earth have taught me otherwise.

What a relief, don't you think?

3

"It's not how far you stretch that matters; it's how much you stretch."

There was a time when I practiced yoga every day. (I'm embarrassed to tell you how long ago *that* was!) Yet for years I took the same beginning class over and over, while the rest of the students continued to advance. No, it wasn't the teacher being prejudiced against me. It was reality. I had terrible health problems, and that beginner status was simply the highest level I could ever achieve.

While it was hard enough that I didn't move forward; worse than that, sometimes I even seemed to be moving backward! In my daily practice, I would often encounter the following very frustrating phenomenon. One day I would be able to stretch to my calves, and the next day I would only be able to reach my knees. It seemed that I was working hard, practicing every day, just to go backwards.

After one of those frustrating episodes, God talked to me about it. He said, "How do you know that it's not harder for you to reach your knees today than it was for you to reach your calves yesterday? How do you know you're not actually stretching more now than then?"

What a novel thought, and what a relief, too. The value of my yoga practice was in the stretch itself, and I might have been stretching more when I seemed to be stretching less. I wasn't failing after all. I was just failing to achieve external results!

I have learned to apply this concept to everything I do in my life, to the many ways I stretch myself emotionally, physically and spiritually every day. I have learned to value the stretch and appreciate my willingness to extend myself, no matter the appearance or end results. And I have learned to apply this aphorism to you, as well.

Let me explain. Sometimes I get intolerant of other people's apparent weaknesses and compare their weaknesses to my strengths. Perhaps, for example, I am more responsible than Joe or more devoted than Mary. Even though I don't know who they are on the inside and I don't know their struggles, I automatically judge them as not trying very hard.

Is it true? Maybe. Maybe not. It's true that I *appear* to be making a greater effort, because I have achieved a greater effect. But maybe it is a greater stretch for Joe to be semi-responsible than it is for me to be totally responsible. And perhaps Mary's minimal devotion is a greater stretch for her than my maximum devotion is a stretch for me.

"It's not how far you stretch that matters; it's how much you stretch." Yes. This aphorism helps me stop judging myself. And if I can do that for myself, perhaps I can stop judging you too.

4

"You had better start liking the process, because that's all there is. Everything is a transition to the next transition."

I don't know about you, but I'm always looking for life to get "better" and for me to get more comfortable. I want to settle into some easier place of being. But instead, life seems to be just a series of lessons and transitions. The challenges never seem to stop.

One day I was asking for divine guidance on some issue, and, of course, in the back of my head was the unasked question: Well, if I do "this", will I get better, and will my life get easier, more comfortable or more secure?

That's when my friend upstairs hit me with this zinger: "You had better start liking the process, Beth, because that's all there is."

What an awful thought. Did this statement mean that from now to eternity, I would be out on the stormy ocean with constant turbulence? Did it mean that I would never "arrive?"

God taught me this aphorism well over twenty years ago, and guess what? I haven't arrived yet. I am still constantly changing and learning, and, if anything, the process has sped up over the past few years. And darned uncomfortable it sometimes is.

What to do?

Well, if I can't stop the process, I'd better learn to enjoy it. And that's what I've done.

First, I've realized that my going through mini-crisis after mini-crisis doesn't make me bad, sick or not spiritual enough. Growth is a never-ending process. So if I'm constantly challenged and learning, it's not because there's anything wrong with me! It's because I'm growing. To think there's something wrong with me because I keep growing is like thinking there's something wrong with a tree for continuing to reach for the sky!

Second, I've realized that life itself is a never-ending evolution, so there's no way to stop new challenges and the need to grow through them. Life just keeps throwing new curves. A teenager has challenges to face around developing skills for living independently; but then the elderly face equal challenges in the face of failing capacities and the loss of independence.

The process of growth is a power greater than I am. It's a part of the universal dynamic, and it's dumb to try to fight it. In fact, instead of fighting it, I can actually learn to appreciate what it offers.

And what it offers is great, because the process of growth is its own reward. After all these years, for instance, I can look back on my own life with awe. When I picture the person I was when God zapped me with this aphorism, I see a confused scared young woman who felt lost. Today I see a much more mature, still confused, but definitely more relaxed and wiser older crone.

Yeah, it's been tough going through the experiences that have gotten me here, but that's my investment in me! And I'm worth it. And guess what? As I sit here this moment, I also know that I am in transition again. Oops, where did she go?

5

"When in doubt, don't."

Now doesn't that sound simple? If you're unsure of what to do, don't do anything. Get quiet and wait for guidance. Or wait till other things fall into place and then you'll intuitively know what to do. Or investigate further, until you have the information you need.

For this kid over here, it's not always so easy. When I feel unsure of what to do, I feel anxious. Since I want to reduce my anxiety, I think the best course is to take action, the illogical logic being that if I make a decision, any decision, at least I won't feel unsure anymore, and if I don't feel unsure, then I will no longer feel anxious.

Ha! What a mistake that is.

Most of the time when I'm anxious, I rush into making a quick decision just to give myself a path to walk, just to relieve the stress. But that quick decision might create headaches for me that could last for years. So now I've traded years of trouble for a moment's relief. And the relief only lasts a moment, because it is immediately followed by even more anxiety, because now that I've made a potentially wrong choice, I really have something to feel anxious about. And I'll have the extra anguish of feeling stupid, because I know I did it to myself. Not a good trade.

What should I do when I feel anxious about a decision? It doesn't hurt to stop, breathe and self-examine. It doesn't hurt to admit that if I'm feeling anxious, I must be having some doubts.

When in doubt, don't act just to relieve anxiety; but do become more conscious. Maybe my doubt is telling me I'm truly not sure what's best. So if I'm still in doubt, I shouldn't try to rush things. (Rush things? Who? me?) Maybe my anxiety is a subtle message from the universe that there is something wrong and that I shouldn't leap in. (You mean I shouldn't marry the guy, even though we've been engaged for two years?) Maybe the doubt is pointing to something unresolved in ME that I need to resolve in order to be clear and make a good decision. (You mean I have to work on myself?) Maybe I feel very overwhelmed by the issue and need to get help to make the best decision. (You mean I can't intuitively know what to do in every situation, and I might need more information?)

I know there are people who procrastinate forever, and they will need to look at that. But for me, I'm more of a leaper than a looker, and anxiety is a friend from heaven telling me that I have some doubts and need to look deeper into what I'm about to do and why.

It's amazing. If I acknowledge my anxiety, admit my doubts and examine my fears and motives, I'll take the steps necessary to more calmly and clearly examine my choices. If I more calmly examine my choices, I'll probably make better decisions, or I'll realize that it's not time to make this decision at all!

Whatever I choose, my decisions may ultimately lead to pain anyway. Whoever said pain could be avoided? But at least my choices wouldn't have been based on anxiety, and I will be able to look myself in the eye with the knowledge that I did the best I could with what I knew.

And that's worth a lot.

6

"God is as close to you as the nose on your face, because God is the nose on your face, because together we are God."

Let's take a minute to start talking about who God is, since she's so free with her advice. Our conversation about God is going to continue throughout this book, but for now let's make a start.

Some people feel really close to God, but to a lot of folks, God is just an abstract idea, a fearful icon from childhood, or an irrelevancy.

I understand that. I've had my own love/hate relationship with God. But let me tell you about the God I connect to—the one who is as close to me as the nose on my face.

My God told me that I am a part of her, and she exists within me. There is no separation. Does that mean that I, alone, am God? No, it means that we, all of us, together, are God—the totality of all being.

I like that. It's inclusive of male and female (which is why I alternately refer to God as he and she). It's inclusive of the light and the dark, the so-called good and bad, every aspect of everything that exists, that has existed and that will ever exist. Every part of me, the good, the bad and the ugly. Every part of everything, the good, the bad and the ugly. Everything is part of God, because everything is part of the totality.

So if I accept that definition, sure I can see that God is the nose on my face, and on your face, and on the face of every monkey in the jungle.

And accepting that definition, I can see that there's no need to search for God or strive to be good for God, because as long as I exist, I am close to God, because God and I are one.

Now let's relax into that one.

7

"Under stress, we regress."

This statement is not a criticism. It's an observation of a natural phenomenon. So if it's natural, let's not criticize ourselves for it.

We work hard to develop healthier patterns of thought and behavior, and then we get hit by a car, a pink slip, or an "I want a divorce" speech from our wife of 25 years. Well, whap, we're now acting like idiots, deep in depression, out of control, yelling, crying or compulsively eating.

Let's not get bent out of shape because of this behavior. It's perfectly normal.

Stress causes us to regress into our default behavior, which are the patterns that have been programmed into us. Sometimes we just have the urge to regress, but good sense saves us. For example, I've been sober from alcohol for two years, but suddenly the thought crosses my mind that "Maybe a drink would taste really good. Where did I see that liquor store?" If I'm lucky, this thought is fleeting, followed by, "Nah, drinking is deadly for me. I think I'll pass."

But then at another point, the stress is stronger than we are, and we might jump in whole hog, before good sense can get in our way. The margarita is already slithering down my throat before I've even noticed my thought process.

Similarly, sometimes we just *want* to bite somebody's head off, but we're able to intervene with ourselves and bite our own tongue instead. At other times we're shocked to see ourselves yelling irrationally, even though we know better. Oh, yeah, brave me, screaming at the puppy for pooping on the carpet for the umpteenth time!

Whether we act out our regression or just wish we could, our behavior is forgivable. We've just hit a stress we couldn't handle. That's all.

Sure we've been trying to learn different behavior, and maybe we've even had some successes. But when we're into our old mode, it's because the stressor is stronger than our new learning. It overwhelms us. It's like trying to contain a tornado in a teacup; the teacup lacks the capacity.

Without sufficient mental/emotional capacity to deal with a stress, we jump back into default mode. It's as simple as that.

So, okay, I acknowledge that I've lost it. Now what? Should I beat myself up? Will that increase my capacity to cope? Of course not. In fact the opposite is true. If I beat myself up, I will become more stressed and will be even less able to handle whatever stressed me to start with!

The best antidote to regression is compassion for myself. That will help me relax again, delve into why I got so stressed and determine what, if anything, I can do about it. Maybe I was too tired or hungry, maybe I felt really threatened, maybe I felt unloved, or maybe I'm just still immature. Ultimately, whatever the circumstances that precipitated my regression, I know I need to do more work on strengthening myself and learning to relax around the stresses of life, whatever they are.

It's natural to regress to old behavior, but it's not required that we stay there. If you catch yourself regressing, give yourself a hug, appreciate your pain, shower yourself with enough love to calm down and relax, and then take your hand and lead yourself back to higher ground.

Boy it feels much better up here.

8

"If you don't reveal it, you can't heal it."

I've heard people say that if you can't feel it, you can't heal it, and they are so right. But if you don't reveal it, you can't heal it either. I've been an intuitive counselor since 1980, and I've seen over and over that keeping things bottled up only makes them stronger and more potent.

Remember high school science? For every action, there is an equal and opposite reaction? The more we try to suppress something within us, the more energy it exerts back, and the more energy we need to suppress it again.

Why are we reluctant to reveal things from the past? Sometimes it's because we, ourselves, are afraid to remember, fearing that remembering will bring up feelings we can't endure. Usually, though, it's not fear but shame that blocks us. As a counselor, I've seen that most of us are trying to bury an experience, because, deep down, we feel we did something wrong, and we're ashamed. Deep down, I believe, yes, it was my fault that mom hit me, that the neighbor raped me or that my sister died in that car accident.

It's no different with current behaviors and feelings. I don't want to reveal them because I'm afraid of the pain or shame, and again shame seems to be the stronger motivator. Let's say I don't want to admit to my husband that I'm having an affair. Sure I may be afraid he'll leave me. But scratch the surface, and you'll see that I also feel ashamed of myself, ashamed of what I see as my betrayal of him or of my attraction to a man half my age or with half my income.

Shame, shame, go away. Don't come back another day. What is shame anyway? It's the sense that there is something wrong with *us*. We feel shame *not* because of what we DO, but because of who that behavior indicates we ARE. We think that our behavior proves that we're selfish, careless, mean, envious, greedy, weak, stupid, perverted, something that makes us look bad in our eyes or the eyes of others. And so we have to hide it. Yet if we explore our behaviors, motives and feelings, we discover they we're not bad; we're just human. We may not make the best choices, but we aren't monsters or intrinsically bad. Our choices are motivated by pain or fear, just like everyone else's.

I still do things that I wish I hadn't. But these days, I reveal them. I'm much less concerned with protecting my ass than healing my heart, so the specter of shame no longer dominates me. When push comes to shove, I want to be at peace with myself, and that takes the courage to reveal.

When our shameful behavior is revealed, our self-condemnation can be healed. We can understand our choices as human, and we can ask for forgiveness, if appropriate, or make amends, if possible. And the most fun of revealing ourselves is the discovery that we're not alone. When we bring out our shameful behaviors in a group, we inevitably find that others are like us. Okay, you may be the only one in the group who's had sex with a chicken, but you won't be the only one whose desperation has led them to insanity.

The power of compassion. The power of recognizing how alike we really are. Revealing myself may be scary, but it's worth it. On this one, I'm with God. Let's reveal it and heal it.

9

"Don't take responsibility for something that isn't yours, in order to avoid taking responsibility for something that is."

Busted! When God first shared this aphorism, he was talking about a client of mine. Yes, I could see this very clearly about her. She was taking responsibility to get her husband to stop drinking and was ignoring her own compulsive eating. She was bossing around others, yet was out of control herself. Glad it wasn't me God was addressing.

But of course it was me, and you, and you, and you. Pretty much all of us do this. We have lots of opinions about what others should do, and we often try to organize them to do it. We try to make others see the light, tow the line and generally behave.

But are we focusing on them instead of ourselves? Absolutely.

Of course, when we're correcting others, we like to choose areas where we at least *seem* to be functioning. This way we can feel truly righteous and hope that nobody notices our lack of self-responsibility. But what's the reality?

Let's take a look at something I've done. I would overwork with clients, trying to help them get well and in the process totally trash my own health. I was taking full responsibility for their healing and avoiding taking any responsibility for my own. And everyone thought I was a hero. Pretty slick.

Or let's say I have a teenager whose behavior is out of control. I righteously lecture, yell, reprimand, wring my hands and obsess. My health goes down the tubes. I walk around gripped with fear.

If I were taking responsibility for myself, I would be asking myself about my own out-of-control behavior, which is me spending hours of my time wringing my hands, lecturing, yelling and obsessing. I would ask myself why I'm so invested in controlling the kid, what feelings of my own I'm trying to fix.

Need I say more?

When I'm stressed and feeling put upon, maybe I should consider this little aphorism. Perhaps I should ask myself if I am taking on responsibilities that are truly mine, or if I'm just borrowing yours, so that I can avoid my own.

10

"Let your light shine so that others might more clearly see their own."

I love this one. It's such an antidote to false modesty.

I've often feared that people wouldn't like me if I put myself forward in a positive light. I feared that they would judge me as full of myself. I feared that they might feel bad about themselves.

Now here's the truth. They may have all these unpleasant reactions, and if they do, that's their problem. But here's another truth. I can't keep myself small in order to make others look big, feel good or like me. That's an insult to us all.

And beyond that, I understand something else. The greater I am, the more I can offer others; the more I can support them to see their own light.

When I feel good about myself, I don't compete with others and have no need to make them feel small. When I feel good about myself, I am more able to share with others how great I think they are. And when I feel good about myself, I have an abundance of love to give to all.

When my light shines, I feel calm, relaxed and capable. I feel like everything will be all right. I am able to allow others to do what *they* need to do, rather than try to force them to do what *I* need them to do—because I don't need them to do anything! My wellbeing is not dependent on what they do or don't do.

When my light shines, I don't need to blow out the lights of others to make mine look more powerful.

When my light shines, I don't need to shame others for having needs and desires that might conflict with my plans for them and us! On the contrary, I can support them to be who they are. I can support their light.

When my light shines, I don't feel inadequate, and so I don't need to compete with others and try to keep them down. Instead, I have the wisdom, ability and desire to support others to reach their potential.

When my light shines, I am an inspiration to others. They look at me and say, "I can do that, too."

I say thank you, God, for my light and for the encouragement to let it shine. And I say thank you, God, for the sense of wellbeing that grows within me every day, that allows me to look at my fellows and appreciate their light, that allows me to give up the need to compete with their light, that allows me to support them to expand their light, so that their light can shine upon me and allow me to more clearly see my own.

11

"If you're meant to be with someone, you will—even if they live far away; if you're not meant to be with them, you won't—even if they live next door."

First let me explain that this aphorism has a lot of applications. Regarding relationships, for example, God is referring to all the "even ifs," such as "even if" the guy is married, leaving town, thinking you're as insignificant as a mosquito in August, or whatever seems like an obstacle that can't be overcome.

What this aphorism tells me is that I can and need to relax into life. I can't twist myself into a pretzel in order to manipulate my fate. It won't work. And I don't have to twist myself into a pretzel, because it's not necessary.

"Even ifs" refer to obstacles that are external and outside my control. But this technique of dealing with the "even ifs" can be applied to me in the form of "even thoughs." Let me show you what I mean.

I have had debilitating health problems all my life. When I've had to introduce myself to a potential date, I could have gotten clutched. "Well, Joe, I'm a great woman, even though I've barely been able to get out of a chair for the last twenty years; and even though I can't stand the smell of flowers, much less your deodorant; and even though etc., etc."

Do I worry about these "even thoughs?" Believe it or not, I don't, because I say, "If he's the right man, he'll want me, even though I'm sick; and if he isn't, he wouldn't want me, even if I weren't."

Isn't that a great way to live and feel?

Now that I've touched on how I overcome feeling vulnerable because of my weaknesses, let me tell you that this aphorism applies to my strengths as well. Men are often intimidated by the fact that I'm an intuitive and can see into them. In fact, I've been rejected more for my strengths than for my vulnerabilities.

So do I feel nervous about revealing my strengths to potential dates? Heck no. I say, "If he's the right guy, he'll want me even though I can see into him; and if he's not, he wouldn't want me, even if I couldn't."

This aphorism can apply to lots of other situations, such as getting a job or surviving a hospital stay or just about anything. Here's an example: "If I'm meant to survive, I will, even though George is driving like a maniac; if I'm not meant to survive, I won't, even if he were driving like a pro."

So does this mean I believe in fate? Who cares? This aphorism works. It helps me have faith, relax and enjoy my life. What more can you ask from one little aphorism?

12

"Of all the things you've done in your life, you are your greatest accomplishment."

A long time ago, I joined a dating service, and the questionnaire asked me to specify what I considered to be my greatest accomplishment. I had to ponder. I had written books and music, become a successful intuitive counselor, and helped and influenced many people, and I had done it all despite the daily obstacle of poor health and minimum energy. Was my greatest accomplishment any of those?

After consultation with God, I laughed, because God told me that *I* was my greatest accomplishment. I had lived a life full of trauma and pain, hardship and frustration, and yet I could still smile, be optimistic and care about others. I was my greatest accomplishment, because I had endured and survived as a loving human being.

Wow! What did the rest matter?

And the same can be said for you. The fact that you're reading this book is a testament to the unquenchable hope that still lives in your heart.

Even if this book is useless to you, your delving into it tells me that you still care about yourself, your soul and your sanity.

Life is tough, and it's amazing and sad how little credit we give ourselves for managing to continue to grow in the face of so much pain. Some people learn and evolve, and some seem to crumble into anger, self-hatred and despair. If you're making it through life, perhaps a bit scarred, but with optimism and willingness intact, you're an incredible being in God's book, and you should be seen as an incredible being in your own.

Ultimately there is only one thing that matters or is carried to the grave, and that is who we are on the inside. So instead of judging ourselves by what we've done on the outside, by our successes or failures, by the wellbeing of our children, by the size of our retirement fund, the number of awards on our wall, or even the number of friends we've collected, remember God's words.

"Of all the things you've done in your life, you are your greatest accomplishment."

So be it.

13

"Be informed by the past but guided by the future."

We've been told to live in the now, and what great advice that is! But here God is also telling us to be informed by the past and guided by the future. How do we do this?

First, how are we informed by the past but not dominated by it? Here's a hint. When a situation arises, let's ask ourselves a series of questions: Is this situation really the same? And even if it is, can the results be different?

Let's start with the question: Is this situation really the same, or does it only appear to be the same? Don't assume that every time your mind makes an association, it's actually telling you the truth. You meet a red-headed woman and she rubs you the wrong way. Is it her, or is it just an association, your fear that every redheaded woman with green eyes is going to act just like your first girlfriend?

Now suppose you really have been in a similar situation, as in, she really *is* like your old girlfriend. How do you know whether the outcome will be the same? Could *you* have changed? Are you capable of responding differently? And what difference could that make? Do you want this experience anyway? Is it worth chancing pain to find out if it's right for you, or is this the red light that tells you to stop?

And, finally, are there any other factors in this situation that could create a different outcome, and how do you know?

Now here's where we need to be guided by the future. Despite everything, sometimes something drives us toward an experience, and we don't always know what. Sometimes it's that old, neurotic, I'm going to keep doing the same thing over and over expecting a different result.

But maybe there's a different reason, a reason that has to do with our destiny, our fate.

Oh, there she goes again with that "meant-to-be" stuff. Yeah but maybe there is a destiny calling you.

Remember the time you felt you just had to move to Cincinnati, and you ended up meeting your next husband? He turned out to be a louse, but it was a valuable experience nonetheless. Or remember the time you just felt like walking the dog in the rain, and you slipped on the sidewalk, broke your leg, ended up in the hospital, met a nurse who sang you a song that reminded you of your mother, which made you cry, and suddenly you were able to forgive her, your mother, that is?

Okay, you're rolling your eyes. But these things happen all the time. If we keep our minds and hearts open, we'll hear the beat of the drum that keeps us walking toward the fulfillment of our life's plan. That beat is the future calling us and guiding us. If we don't listen to it, we're likely to cling to the past and smother the present.

Just as the pregnant mom intuitively starts to "nest" and just as the overworked salesclerk drags himself to school every night for 8 years, and just as the elderly woman starts dreaming about her family long dead but waiting for her on the other side, we are called by the future. Whether because common sense guides us or because intuition drives us, we are always preparing for the future. The present is a wonderful moment, but part of what makes it so wonderful is our always looking forward to the transcendence of what already is.

14

"You are the drop of water that's different from all the rest."

One day I was asking God, "Who am I?" And he replied this way:

"Go look into the stream. You are the drop of water that's different from all the rest."

"But that's ridiculous," I protested, because I couldn't even define a drop of water without taking it out of the stream. And, in fact, if I isolated that drop, it would probably evaporate.

"That's my point," he replied.

With those words, I finally got it. I am part of the stream, the collective, a collective made up of all humanity and beyond.

That realization changed my life, because in that moment I understood that we are all connected and that I am part of a larger whole. I also understood that anybody who pisses into the stream will impact everybody downstream. And that includes me.

My first reaction was a bit of shock. You mean I'm not special? But soon that reaction changed. I felt happy to be a part of something bigger. It gave me a place in the universe.

This new perspective let me relax. So much of my life and my energy had been spent trying to distinguish myself, trying to prove to myself and others that I was the smartest, or the most dedicated, or the most spiritual, or the most something. How silly.

What's the point of all that striving and struggling to be distinguished from everybody else? At the core of our beings, we're all connected. We all ultimately share the same earth, the same water, the same air and the same fate.

This new perspective also made me feel less like a failure. If the stream is polluted, you can't keep your own drop clear, right? So how could I feel perfectly happy and peaceful in a world full of pain and fear? How could I ever become the perfect individual I thought I was supposed to become? I couldn't. And it wasn't my fault.

And, finally, this perspective made me realize my accountability to everybody. If I want to be well emotionally, physically and spiritually, not only do I have to take care of myself, I have to help clear the stream.

But all I have to do is my part.

I can do that.

15

"You can't clean the air over one house in Los Angeles."

Most of us spend our lives trying to help and fix our "selves." But it doesn't work, because we are not individual selves, we're part of a whole, part of the web of life.

I once lived in a U.S. city in a poor, working class neighborhood and worked in the very polluted downtown area. The river, which ran through downtown, was so dirty, it actually burned. The wealthy folk, who owned the industries that polluted the river that poisoned the rest of us, lived in the suburbs. They enjoyed their beautiful, pristine communities, and they weren't suffering.

Not at first, but the chickens will come home to roost. Eventually, the pollution got so bad, it reached them too, and suddenly some of the rich and powerful put out a call for environmental responsibility. Only when they suffered the consequences of their actions did they care to do anything about them.

We can't remain forever isolated from the consequences of our collective behavior. No matter how rich you are, if you live in Los Angeles, you'll have unhealthy air. And you can't clean the air over only your own house. You'll have to protect everybody's air. You can try to escape by living at the ocean, of course, but unless you never leave the house, you'll share the environment with the rest of us.

If we can't fix one house's environment, we also are limited in fixing ourselves. If we are all connected, our thoughts and feelings will affect one another. If we live in a society that is sick, it's hard for any of us to feel well.

Do we live in a society that's emotionally and spiritually polluted? You tell me. Young girls are starving themselves, and everybody has plastic surgery for imaginary imperfections. Lots of folks are convinced they need a perfect body, a perfect face, lots of money and the trendiest this and that to be loved and validated. We must be pretty miserable to drive ourselves in these ways.

Many of us realize we're unhappy and try to fix our "selves." We read inspiring books, try self-help programs and spend tons of money on therapy and psychiatric drugs. These may help us as individuals, but they don't change the fact that your kid could be shot by a depressed schoolmate, your boss is unreliable because she's on drugs, your partner is stressed to the max, and you're scared to drive because of the nuts on the freeway.

As a society, we lack love, compassion, a sense of belonging, validation and connection. And where can we get them? Not from a culture that focuses on "me, me, me."

So while we're desperately trying to fix our "selves," we can't. We're not individual selves, and there is no personal salvation. To be truly well, we need to change "us."

This is the reality of our world, too. No one is safe behind the fortress of the illusion that we are separate. A virus that starts in a slum in Bangkok will end up killing your next-door neighbor. AIDS is ravaging people around the world. And poor workers abroad will steal your job.

The sooner we recognize we are one world and one consciousness, the sooner we will realize that we need to support one another, the sooner we will all achieve the greater sense of peace and wellbeing that we crave.

Can we do it? What else do we have to do?

16

"You are not your brother's keeper; you are your brother."

Ooh, that hurts. Here I thought I was being such a good person by showing concern for those less fortunate than I. Now I'm being told that I AM the person who is less fortunate than I. Now that's confusing.

It's that oneness stuff again. Just about all spiritual traditions tell us that we are one in God or something to that effect. Are they serious?

God told me that each one of us is like a cell in the body of the whole, which some of us call God. So, maybe I'm a finger cell and maybe you're a toe cell. But we're all fundamentally the same and have the same spiritual DNA, because we're all connected, all cells of the body of God.

So what does that mean anyway?

Let's go back to the idea of the finger vs. the toe. If the finger casually chops off the toe, it won't be laughing for long. Hey, we could all bleed to death or get an infection.

Now look at this. We actually feel one another's feelings. Yes, we do. If I go into a room where everyone is anxious, nine times out of ten, I'll feel anxious, too. If you're sad and we're in the same room, I'll feel the sadness too.

That means, among other things, that I can't hurt you without hurting myself. I've noticed that. My guts do get wrenched when I see your pain. And they get wrenched even more when I know I've caused it.

Feeling one another's pain can cause us to go into denial. I don't like feeling your pain, I don't know what to do about it, and therefore I try to pretend I don't feel it. Or I just try to run away from you, hoping to escape from your feelings. Or I blame you and try to distance myself from you by making you look at fault. Our denial and distancing will often be even more extreme when we feel we've caused the pain. I feel so bad about hurting you that I have to assure myself that it's your fault.

Want an example? Okay. I want to leave my wife after 25 years of marriage. I know she'll be devastated, so I'm already feeling guilty. What to do? Blame her, of course. She didn't do this, or she did do that. Whether or not any of that is true, I'm still trying to blame her, so that I don't have to feel her pain.

Are we really one another? When I look deeply, I see that we are. We're all drops in the same stream, remember? There isn't much about you that I can't identify as existing in myself. You have your pains; I have mine. You have your desires; I have mine. You have your dreams, fears and aspirations; I have mine.

Oh, sure, we're also separate. I have my own energy field and body; and you have yours. And it's also true that you sometimes try to make me responsible for your feelings, which I'm not. But that's another issue. The truth is that spiritually we're one, and we're connected like cells in the same body.

I know that I am fundamentally responsible for myself and my own actions. But if I could remember that we are spiritually one, maybe I wouldn't be so quick to hurt you for my advantage.

After all, I'm only hurting myself.

17

"If you think you create your own reality, try to get somewhere faster when you're stuck in traffic."

I admit it. I have a pet peeve about the concept that you create your own reality. As I've mentioned in earlier sections, I have been seriously ill most of my life, and it really outraged me when some perfectly healthy person would advise me that I had created my own reality. Right!

I used to confront such a person with the following question: Could one person stare out into space and conjure up fast food in the middle of the desert?

Well, God thought that statement was funny too. But maybe the answer is in the question.

Maybe we do create reality, but we do it as a group. Perhaps many people together could bring fast food to the middle of the desert. (You could ask why they would want to, but that's a different question….)

It would take people and resources to bring electricity and water; it would take jobs for there to be enough money to buy the burgers; it might take some convincing to influence people to buy the food; and there would need to be roads. Yes, if we wanted to, we might be able to co-create that reality. Or maybe not. Even together, the goal might be beyond us.

We really co-create everything. This book, for example. Even though I'm the one who wrote it, it took my parents and a community to raise me, a world to feed and clothe me, friends and clients to help me develop my ideas, God to talk to me, tons of people to develop the technology to create the computer that serves me, and how many people to develop and deliver the electricity that powers it all?

Believing that we create our own reality is a good antidote to believing that we're powerless. But the truth is much more complex.

Now I want to share with you what I'd like to co-create—a more peaceful and compassionate world. I can't do it, but maybe *we* can—you me, and God. Of course, I can only do my part, and what is my part? Whatever I can do.

For the rest, I need to let go and see what happens. It can be frustrating to allow the universe to do what it's going to do in the face of so much suffering, but it also relieves me. It means I get to enjoy my life while I'm allowing our fate to play out.

And talking about "in the meantime," in the meantime while I'm stuck in traffic, I might as well acknowledge my powerlessness, relax and turn on some music.

18

"The truth is there is no truth."

Lots of us argue about beliefs and ideas, and that's good, because beliefs are powerful and impact our behavior and our lives. But beliefs are not truths, and we should acknowledge that. Truth is what is, and we have no way of knowing the totality of what is.

Science reveals to us all the time how wrong science was yesterday. Are our opinions about anything else more certain? Let's remember that little parlor game where we all see the same thing and then we're asked to describe it. We discover that we see different things. Or let's think about the story about the three blind men touching different parts of the elephant and arguing about what that elephant is.

Every thought is a concept of the human mind, a way of perceiving reality. So why don't we just acknowledge we're discussing ideas and arguing about perceptions, instead of pretending we're really arguing about truth itself.

The truth is there is no truth. Truth is what is. But we can't know it; what we know is our perceptions, and even our perceptions are not objective. They are influenced by social biases, our own history and reactivity, our training, education and different capacities.

And even if we could know the truth, it changes every moment. Yes the thing we are describing is changing in the moment of our description, because life is always in motion. The cloud you are painting has changed before your brush has reached the easel, and the world we are describing has changed before our opinions have been formed.

Truth is changing and unknowable. So we're left with beliefs. Now what?

Beliefs are ideas, concepts that we create to help us understand and navigate reality. They are useful; but they are not truths.

How freeing is that! If there is no truth, you don't have to know it or convince me of your version. You have a belief that works for you, keep it. If it doesn't work, dump it.

Could it possibly be that simple?

Yes and no. It's scary to realize that we're creating our beliefs, because it makes us more responsible. We now have to evaluate our beliefs and their impact on us and others. Then we have to choose to keep or change them. There's nobody else responsible to do that for us.

Let's take an example. Perhaps I believe that I am master of my own destiny. Does that belief make me strong and courageous, or does it make me arrogant and unrealistic? Does it remind me that I am capable of improving my life, or does it encourage me to beat myself up when I can't control my fate? Do I use this belief to support others to change or to shame them when they can't?

If beliefs aren't truths, we can hold two opposing beliefs at the same time and use each when appropriate. We can believe that we control our own destiny one day and that we're powerless over fate the next, whichever helps us more!

Beliefs are thoughts, just concepts of the mind. But many of us are so identified with them, we can't face this possibility and may even kill to prove ourselves right. The history of the world has more than enough evidence of this.

Okay, the truth is there is no truth. But then, is that true? Sometimes it is, and sometimes it isn't. Fun, isn't it?

19

"Suffering may be an illusion, but it still hurts."

I'm not knocking other people's spiritual belief systems. In fact all systems have value. But for me, the idea that suffering is an illusion just doesn't work, and it causes me more suffering. That doesn't mean that we don't create lots of needless suffering. We certainly do.

Take the teenager who believes that she must get a date with Ricky or she'll die. Okay, a little melodramatic, but to her, it's real. Let's not shame her. The best thing is to hear her out and find out why she feels this way. Maybe she thinks if Ricky doesn't want her, no one ever will. Maybe she doesn't really care about Ricky, but is ashamed to be seen as undesirable in front of the other girls.

Her drama over the date may seem rather foolish to us, yet we've all felt the sting of rejection and humiliation, and many of us have felt we were going to "die" from the shame of not being wanted. Help her see past her pain, but don't shame her for it. Tell her that throughout life, there will be those who like her and those who don't, and their reactions may or may not have anything to do with her. Help her see that ultimately, she will have to like herself, however others feel, or she'll be forever a slave to other people's opinions and behavior. By acknowledging her pain and helping her see past it, you lessen her suffering, because she can go past the reactions that create it.

Sometimes our pain has a real cause from the past. Take the example: If I am rejected, I'll die. Maybe we really weren't wanted by our families, and without love and nurturing, we were actually in danger of dying. Though we're adults, and our survival is no longer at stake, we haven't realized that it is now an illusion that rejection equals death. Our pain is real, though the cause isn't.

The longer we live, the more we learn to overcome needless pain. The more conscious we are and the more we understand ourselves, the more we can identify the roots of our suffering and the ways to alleviate it. By gaining perspective and increasing self-love, we actually reduce the illusions that cause needless pain. But we don't do any of this by beating ourselves up.

Physical suffering can also be very difficult to bear. Many of us suffer chronic and/or acute pain, weakness or fatigue that distract us from living and dramatically reduce the quality of our lives. In that there is suffering.

But perhaps this suffering can also be reduced. Perhaps I can be more realistic about my age, condition and activities. Or perhaps I can clear emotional components, such as blaming myself for my pain. For example, if my having driven under the influence caused the auto accident that crippled me, if my diabetes was brought on by sugar addiction, if my illness was brought on by my own neglect, my suffering will be worsened by my judgments of myself. If I know this, I can try to understand myself, accept my past and embrace the realities of my today. My suffering is thereby reduced.

Self-hatred is the cause of the worst of our suffering. So what helps us most is compassion for our suffering, not self-condemnation for experiencing it.

Pain hurts enough. We don't need to add to the pain by shaming ourselves for feeling it.

20

"Your hangnail hurts you more than someone else's broken leg."

How embarrassing to admit this, but what a relief, as well.

Earlier in the book, I talked about oneness and how we are one another and feel one another's pain. And that is true. At the very same time, we are individuals, with our own energy fields, skin, bones and nervous systems. So on another level, my hangnail does hurt me more than your broken leg.

I can watch a catastrophe that's playing out in Asia, southern Africa or in the town right up the road. My heart hurts when I see the images, and I feel that I should do something. And maybe I do make an effort to help others.

But when I turn the television off, I sit down at my desk and realize my back still hurts and I can't pay the rent, I check my email and there's no message from the new love interest, and I get a phone call from my father reminding me that I forgot to pick up his prescription from the pharmacy. My problems, my sadness, my headaches. They may not be as great as a tsunami, but they still hurt.

Our sensitivity to our own pain should not be used as a reason to ignore the reality of others'. Nor should we forget that we are part of humanity and are impacted by what happens to us all. But let's be honest that we feel what we feel, and let's not judge ourselves for it.

Realistically, we need to face that

1. We are very attuned to our own pain and

2. We need to be *educated* about the connection between our pain and everyone else's. We need to be taught consciousness.

In this volume, we've started talking about our oneness and how much our pain is actually connected. But I'd also like to remind us to have compassion for ourselves in the meantime. Sometimes we look downright silly in our little concerns and crises, but our pain is real.

If we can acknowledge that our pains and problems feel big to us, perhaps we can also acknowledge that other people's pains and problems seem equally big to them. Yes, even in our self-centeredness we are connected to one another!

So I can acknowledge that, just as my hangnail hurts me more than your broken leg, your aching feet hurt you more than my aching heart.

Yes we are one.

21

"You can't do the right thing for the wrong reason."

People are always asking me and each other what they should do in this or that situation, but how can we really know what's best?

One thing I've learned along the way is to heed this advice from God, that whenever considering any course of action, *it's not what I do that matters; it's why I do it*. I can't do the right thing for the wrong reason.

From the time I was given this advice by God, I've trained myself to immediately look at my motives in regard to anything I'm doing. If I understand my motives, I can ask myself if I really want to act on that basis. For example, if my motive is to show someone up, I won't take the action, even though the action might look innocent. Understanding my motives also opens me to make the right decision, because it stops me from acting from the wrong basis. I understand myself, deal with my feelings, find a way to let go of my agenda, relax, open myself to guidance and automatically make better choices.

Checking out our motives, rather than relying on our ability to predict outcomes, makes a lot of sense. First of all, only God knows what will happen, and maybe even he doesn't know. Example: You have a teenage child who is in rebellion, and you're trying to determine whether to be tough or forgiving. Which will have the better outcome? You can argue that the child has abused your kindness before, and it's time for tough love. Or you can argue that the child needs you to keep faith with her and sooner or later that faith will bear fruit. But do you really know? Of course not. If you try to base your decision on the outcome, you can't, and if the outcome turns out to be the opposite of what you expected, you take it out on the kid for making you look like a fool!

Another reason to examine our motives is that our motives themselves impact an outcome. Let's go back to the teenager. Supposing your kid is making you look bad in front of yourself and others. You might be embarrassed that you can't control her behavior, because it makes you look weak or mean. Your urge to get tough may really be motivated by your desperate need to look powerful; or your urge to be forgiving might be motivated by your need to look good.

Either way, the child senses your motive and reacts to it. "Yeah, man, my dad wants me to straighten up, not because he loves me, but because he wants to look good in front of mom or his friends." Or "Dad wants to look like a hero. I know how to get *him*. I'll act out even worse."

Giving up our agenda opens us to making better decisions. Regarding our teen again, once you've self-examined and let go of the need to look good and/or powerful, you're more relaxed, more able to think and feel, and more open to real guidance. You'll pick up a clue somewhere—from the radio or a friend—and suddenly you know what to do for your teen. While you don't know the outcome, you know one thing: that when you stop trying to manipulate for your own advantage, you give your kid an example of honesty and accountability. You're impacting her future not by correcting her, but by correcting yourself.

When I stop doing things for the wrong reasons, I still may not like the outcome. But I can predict one thing, the impact on me: I become more the person I want to be.

22

"Don't worry today about what you can worry about tomorrow."

This one gave me a good laugh. My mother has got to be one of the world's most intense worriers, and I inherited the gene.

Suppose I'm taking a trip next week. She will worry now about whether or not I'll get there safely then, how the weather will be at that time, and will I find the house flooded when I return. And she'll worry about whether I'll call when I get there and when I get home. In other words, she is worrying now about the fact that she's going to worry later. Remember, I haven't even left yet!

But it doesn't end there. Knowing my mother is going to worry about me, I worry about her worrying. So I'm already worried. And when next week comes, instead of focusing on getting to my destination safely and having a good time, I'm worrying about getting to a phone to reassure her that there's nothing to worry about.

Worry is not a sign of love, although many of us think it is. And it certainly does no one any good. It just causes stress.

Mom and I can joke about this, and that's the saving grace, of course. But worry can kill joy. While she's worrying that she's going to worry, she's not happy. When she's worrying, she's not happy. And when I'm worrying about her worrying, I'm not happy either.

Worry is not a virtue. It is a waste of our life force. It does not make us responsible. It just makes us tense. In fact, it makes us less capable of coping with whatever problems do arise. To deal with the inevitable glitches of daily life, we need to be relaxed, alert and creative. If we're tense with worry, we're the opposite

When I'm honest, I realize that I can get addicted to worry. There's a kind of adrenaline rush about it. So since worry is not a virtue, but rather an addiction, I think I'd better listen to God. Evaluate when it's appropriate to start taking action about something and when it's time to think about it. Start worrying then.

Because it was about her, I just read this aphorism to mom. When she heard me say that worry was an addiction that needed to be overcome, she said, "Beth, you've taken the joy out of my life." We had a good laugh.

23

"First you run from the dark; then you run toward the light."

This is a wonderful gift I've gained from my spiritual journey—the shift from growing because of the pain to growing because of the love of it. Don't get me wrong. For as many years as I've been working on myself, I still change because old patterns are painful; but now I want to.

Growth feels good. I feel proud of myself and my inner achievements. And I enjoy the excitement, the self-love and the sense of empowerment that come along with it.

The catalyst to my spiritual growth was the drinking of a boyfriend. I started seeking help and was advised to go to a 12-step program devoted to people just like me. I thought they would tell me how to stop his addiction. Of course, instead, they helped me confront my own. I had to look at my need to try to control the universe and mold it according to my vision. And I began to release the pain and fear that motivated this behavior.

The 12-step programs suggest there's a power greater than ourselves. I had been an atheist most of my life up to that point (this was 1978), and I almost bolted at that idea. But when I looked around the room, I noticed that the people there looked a lot happier than I. Maybe they knew something I didn't.

That was the beginning, the beginning of a spiritual journey that has changed me more than I could have imagined, a journey that has brought me emotional, mental and energetic healing.

I love it. One by one I have confronted the painful reactions and self-destructive behaviors I had developed over my life. Every day, life has thrown me another zinger, which has been an opportunity to confront myself again and to gain more relief. Sometimes the process of change seems to have happened in a snap; other times, it seems to have dragged out forever. But it always feels better on the other side.

I still change because of pain, but now I do it with a lot more grace and a lot more tools and inner capacity. Let's say I'm feeling pain, and it's hard to fathom that there is anything I can do to alter my state. I think that circumstances have to change for me to feel better. Circumstances don't change. There's no way out. I feel as though I will explode. Then I remember to go toward the light. I open myself to the possibility that maybe the one who has to change is me. I want to, I can, and I do, even if it takes a long time.

I have healed enough so that I have a paradigm of inner change to rely on. I have tools, skills and new spiritual ideas. I don't resist much anymore, and this whole process can sometimes move with lightning speed

How far do I have to go in my growth? As far as I can. I love being a more balanced, compassionate and realistic person. And I love making fewer and fewer dumb choices based on addictive patterns of thought. I like myself more and more every day, and I like life more too.

I started my spiritual journey hoping to control another person. Now I know true joy comes from regulating myself, behaving in ways that make me feel good about me and having the ability to laugh at myself when I can't!

I love growth. It gives me peace and self-respect. Yup, first I was running from the dark, but now I run toward the light. Catch me if you can!

24

"You can't lose what you don't have."

One day when I was in meditation, I saw myself flying above my home. At that point God said to me, "Do you see that house down there? That's yours to enjoy but not to own." Then he showed me my then husband and said, "Do you see that man down there. He is yours to enjoy but not to own." And finally God lifted me above the earth and says, "Do you see that planet down there. It's yours to enjoy but not to own."

I own nothing, not even my own life. It's a gift, and I can't clutch it.

I've had to laugh at myself many times in this regard. I'm bent out of shape because a relationship is not working out the way I want it to. Do I own it? Do I own the person I'm in relationship with? Am I losing it, or did I never have it to begin with?

I'm afraid I'm going to lose a job I haven't gotten yet, a vacation I haven't yet taken, a opportunity to be loved or appreciated, a chance to appear on the radio, a book deal, a new client, and so on and so on.

How can I be losing these things? I don't have them.

This aphorism applies to everything in my life. I have a belief that I am supposed to have enough money, a life partner, the house I want, a puppy that doesn't piddle on the carpet, a car that never breaks down and perfect health. Ha! Where did I get the idea that these things are mine to have?

I have to have; I have to do; I have to get. And the most deadly "have to" is the idea that I have to have control.

Here's an example. I'm an intuitive counselor and self-employed. Sometimes I'm so busy I can't handle it; other times business seems to evaporate.

Do I have to have the schedule and income I've decided is my right? Can I control the flow of my life? The needs of my clients? Reality tells me no, regardless of my desire to control.

Although I am responsible for my life, I have amazingly little control over its flow. Yet there's some good news here, too. Regarding work, for instance, if I let go, a solution arises, even if it's a solution I don't like. When I'm too busy, three clients will call and have to reschedule. When I'm not busy enough, I get a migraine that lasts until my next appointment.

Does this lack of control equal disaster? No. For reasons I still cannot fathom, even if I work less, I usually seem to have just enough money to manage. If I don't, it's time to re-evaluate my expenses.

To release that clutching feeling, I need to realize that I am not losing control of my life, because I can't lose what I don't have. I don't have control of my life and never will.

And there's more good news. If I can't lose what I don't have, how can I not have what is mine? The job that belongs to me, I will get. The opportunities that are mine will come. The man who has my name on him will arrive, or not. And nothing else. Believing this helps me relax and enjoy.

God lifts me above myself and says, "Do you see that woman down there, Beth. Her life is yours to enjoy, but not to own." Yes.

25

"We are all molesters."

During my years as an intuitive counselor, I've worked with many people who have been sexually molested, as well as those who have molested others themselves. And what God has taught me is that the molester is a person who exploits someone else's vulnerability to hide their own.

Guess what? On some level, we all molest, not necessarily sexually, but in other ways.

First let's take a look at the example of the child molester. Why would I molest? I probably feel pretty inadequate about myself and/or my sexuality. I feel that a woman will ridicule, reject or control me. I want to feel powerful, so I seduce a child, a child who will either fear or respect me, a child who lacks the ability to compare me to other lovers or to make me feel small.

Because I feel vulnerable, I pick someone even more vulnerable, whose vulnerability I can exploit. But when I exploit them, I know it, which causes me shame. I hate myself and/or desperately try to rationalize my behavior. I feel like a weakling, and I need to molest again to prove how powerful I am.

We all feel powerless in some and in many arenas of our lives. Instead of working to strengthen those weaknesses, we often try to hide them from ourselves and others. What better way than to exploit other people's vulnerabilities? To create feelings of shame in them?

How do we all do this? Perhaps I have more self-discipline than a friend. Do I lord it over them that I control my diet, and they can't? Am I picking a very vulnerable spot of theirs to make the comparison with great, big me?

Or let's say I'm a successful businessman. Do I flaunt my success, so that others feel inadequate? Or, if I'm a fortunate parent, do I brag about my children to a couple whose kids are having trouble in school?

Counselors and therapists have a huge responsibility to avoid molesting our clients. Aside from the obvious danger of a sexual relationship with a person in a vulnerable role, we have to beware of many other opportunities to exploit clients' vulnerability. Am I using them to look smart, feel powerful, gain validation or praise? Do I do this by constantly reminding them how much they need me? Do I try to make them dependent on me emotionally, in order to hide that I am dependent on them for validation and income?

Probably one of the most dangerous terrains for all of us is our love relationships, where we are familiar with one another's vulnerabilities and know just where to thrust the knife. How easy it is to hide how vulnerable I am to you by making you feel how vulnerable you are to me. I can mock you, threaten to leave you, or point out your weaknesses as a breadwinner or a lover. How powerful I feel when I put you down. How much more powerful I feel when I don't.

When we have molested another, whether it's a lover, friend, employee, child or anyone else in our lives, we know it, we feel it, and we feel shame for having done it. Now we feel even worse about ourselves, and we have an even stronger need to molest.

The more we acknowledge our vulnerabilities, the more conscious we are of our tendency to molest one another, the less likely we are to do it, the more powerful we feel, and the less we need to molest again.

26

"Never say behind someone's back what you wouldn't say in front of their face."

Gossip is painful. It hurts the person we gossip about, and it hurts us. And, most of all, it poisons our relationships.

Is talking about someone always gossip? Of course not. One legitimate purpose for talking about someone is to clear our own feelings. For example, if I'm really angry at my wife, I may need to talk to someone about it, so that I can get clear about why I'm angry. When I understand my own anger, I can either change myself, discuss it with her and/or leave the relationship.

Or maybe we need to strategize and get support in figuring out what to do in a situation. Let's say I'm annoyed with a co-worker. I might need to talk to someone about how to approach him. Or sometimes when I'm concerned about a friend, I need to share that concern with someone who can help me get clear about how I can help.

If we're not doing one of these things—getting clear about our feelings, our approach or how we can help—chances are we're gossiping. Gossip is an addiction. It's an instant fix to make us feel better about ourselves. In that sense, it's a form of molest. We're exploiting someone else's vulnerability (some behavior of theirs that makes them look bad) to make ourselves look better. But ultimately it makes us feel worse.

How does gossip hurt others? Obviously it spreads a negative belief about the person we're gossiping about. How does it hurt us? It makes us feel ashamed. And how does it hurt our relationship? Because we can't look that other person in the eye without remembering how we took advantage of their weakness to make ourselves look good in the eyes of ourselves and others.

And what about the person we're gossiping with? How dirty do they feel? Let's say I tell Harry that I think Charles is stealing money from the till, but I don't want him to talk to Charles because I have no actual proof. Harry's relationship with Charles gets disrupted, because now Harry has information about Charles that he can't verify with him.

Gossiping to Harry about Charles' stealing gives Harry permission to gossip to me about Charles' sex life. Plus Harry may discuss Charles' stealing with Sally. By gossiping with Harry, I've fed his tendency to gossip as well. Now we have an epidemic.

Gossip doesn't always "look" negative. It could "look" like concern or sympathy. But use the acid test. Will you immediately go to the person you're discussing and share your feelings directly? If not, it's gossip.

"Never say behind someone's back what you wouldn't say in front of their face" means that, before I open my mouth to Mary about Jill, I know that I will ultimately have to talk to Jill about it as well, so I'll think twice before I talk with Mary. Of course I may want to rationalize my way out of talking to Jill directly. But with this aphorism in my mind, chicken or not, I have no way out.

Following this guideline creates feelings of trust. You can rest assured that once I've talked to someone else about you, I'll talk to you about it right after. This keeps our relationship clean, and that's a gift in itself.

27

"If you want to keep something secret, don't do it."

One day I was talking with a group of friends about my reaction to someone's behavior. It was my husband's, and everyone knew it. It was important for me to get support around my reactions. But what about his right to privacy?

That's when God laid this aphorism on me. My husband hadn't asked me to keep his behavior secret, but I knew he felt ashamed of it. Did I create the shame by talking about it? Or did he create the shame by doing it?

Of course some secrets should be kept, such as I'm planning a surprise party for you. Or, I'm on a humanitarian mission for the United Nations that could jeopardize thousands if it were known. But few secrets are in that category. Mostly we keep secrets because we've done something we think is wrong, or we believe someone else will think is wrong. And we don't want the consequences.

What are the consequences that scare us? That someone will think less of us or punish us for our behavior. But there's a better solution than secrecy. If I feel drawn to do something I think is wrong, rather than keeping it a secret, I'd rather get the support to not do it. And if I've done it already, it's the amends, not the secrecy, that will clear my conscience and make me feel better about myself. If I'm still afraid of punishment, I need to remember that my self-contempt is the worst punishment of all, and I can't respect myself until I've made amends.

If I think something is right, I don't want to keep it a secret, even if someone else might disapprove. If my parents don't approve of my choice of men, they may disown me. But if I want to keep my self-respect, I'll have to take that chance. If my employer disapproves of my way of working but I think that it's right, I need to do it their way or disagree openly and risk losing my job. If I do it my way behind their back, I live with the anxiety of getting caught.

It's a lot easier to follow this aphorism as an adult than as a child, of course. If you're a child and your parents tell you to do something you think is wrong, or if they want to prevent you from doing something you think is right, you're in a bind, because you have very little control over your life

But most of us have choice and keep secrets because we're just lacking in the courage to face the music. You want to cheat on your wife and you don't want her to know, because you like your comfortable life. You say you don't want to tell her, because she'll be upset, but you know that's a self-serving rationalization. Best to tell her before the affair that you're attracted to another woman and discuss what's causing you to be available to others. If you want to work it out with her, try. Maybe suggest therapy. If you've already had the affair, fess up and go on from there. If you don't want to work it out, be honest and let her express her anger. Take the consequences.

We like to manipulate what people know about us because we don't want to accept the consequences of our behavior. But we'll always feel ashamed if we cop out, and that consequence is the worst. And we will have destroyed any possibility of relationship with the person we're betraying or lying to. Intimacy is based on self-revelation. We can't build it on a lie.

28

"A love relationship is not a 50-50 proposition; each partner gives 100% of what they have."

This aphorism makes me laugh, because it stops me from puffing myself up about all I give and takes the comparison out of what each of us does. Instead, it guides us to examine what each one of us has to give to a relationship, and then leads us to ask "Are we giving it?"

How would you measure 50-50 anyway? Comparing is tricky. Generally speaking, we tend to be more aware of our own contributions than our partners', just as we tend to be more aware of our pain. (Remember? My hangnail hurts more than your broken leg.) So we may be blind to reality.

Second, unless we're comparing apples with apples, how do we compare fairly? In the classic example, we have the traditional marriage where the man would get home from work, ask for a beer and decide his day was done. How do you equalize his earning money with her 24-hour a day job? He might wonder what she had been doing all day until he was left alone with the kids for three hours. But she might not be able to tolerate the stress of his job either. By what measure do you determine 50-50? By power? Prestige? Using those criteria, the money-earner is way ahead.

Fortunately, we've gotten past that prejudice, at least some of us have, and there is much more equality in relationships than there was. But no matter what kind of relationship we have, traditional or nontraditional, how do we compare the value of each contributor? We can't.

When we evaluate our relationship using God's guideline, first we look at ourselves and ask whether or not we are giving to the relationship all we have to give. If I have the capacity to help financially, why am I not? If I have the capacity to give more help with the kids, why am I not? If I have the capacity to give more love, more comfort, more understanding or more compassion, why am I not?

Then we look at our partner. While we can't compare our contributions, we can evaluate whether or not we value what they offer. If we don't, perhaps we shouldn't be there.

If we value what our partner offers but think they're withholding, we need to discuss our feelings with them. But when evaluating whether our partner is giving what he/she has, we have to get honest. Frequently I hear partners saying of each other, "But she doesn't..." or "But he doesn't...." Well, maybe he or she doesn't, and maybe he or she can't. But instead of comparing our partner to some ideal in our head, we need to look honestly at his or her capacities.

If a couple finds that each is withholding from the other, they have a problem. Either each is withholding because they think the other is; or these two people have difficulty giving to one another. Why? Only honest soul-searching can help them sort this out. But instead of starting with why doesn't he, how about starting with, why don't I and go from there?

To feel loved, I have to know that my partner is giving 100% of what he has. And to feel loving, I need to know that I'm doing the same. This doesn't mean I give my all to the relationship. I need to have a life, too. But if I have something to give to a relationship, I need to give it or not be there.

29

"Equality is not about being the same; it's about each partner being and bringing to the relationship the totality of who they are."

This aphorism sounds similar to the last one, but it has its own twist. It's really about equality and respect, and it applies to any kind of relationship.

Let's say I'm the spiritual director of The Stream, a nonprofit organization. I write the books, develop the programs, do the public speaking and support everyone else's work. And let's say that you do support work and help coordinate workshops. You make the phone calls, drive the motorhome, buy the food, register the participants and make sure there's enough candles and toilet paper.

Are we equal? Yes, as long as we both bring the totality of who we are.

I'm good at writing, counseling and developing programs, but I'm physically weak. If we've planned a trip to Los Angeles, and you don't show, I can't go either. How can I do my job, if you don't do yours? Whichever of us counsels and whichever drives, we are equally responsible for the work and the benefit that people hopefully receive.

The same is true of everything else you provide—the warm and efficient registration of participants, the food that keeps me going so I can work, and the quiet ambience of a room filled with candles.

It may be true that it's easier to find someone to do your job than it is to replace me, just because my intuitive skills are more rare. But that's not the point. The point is that if you don't bring the totality of who you are to the job, we will be as unable to accomplish our work as if I took a drink and became incoherent! And, trust me, finding someone to do your job with grace and accountability is wonderful, awesome and rare in and of itself.

In a world where there is a tremendous division of both labor and financial rewards, it's hard for us to keep in mind the equality of value and responsibility. If the doctor goes to operate, but the staff forgot to sterilize the surgical instruments, the patient could die. If you're the one in charge of sterilization, and you don't respect your value, your work and your job, you could be lax and the results could be disastrous.

It's crucial that we each feel our value and keep in mind the impact we have. The person who cleans the house creates a sense of order. The one who fixes the plumbing protects our comfort and health. The one who furnishes the home brings function and aesthetic pleasure. The one who pays the mortgage keeps the wolf from the door. And the children who inhabit the house give it life.

If you want to feel like an equal, act like an equal. Bring into every partnership and relationship the totality of who you are. You will respect yourself more, and very likely others will respect you more as well.

30

"The antidote to disappointment is enlightenment."

We've all had our disappointments. Some of them are large and some small. And they hurt. But the best way to get past the hurt is to allow ourselves to be enlightened.

What do I mean by enlightenment? Bringing light, or awareness, to everything that I experience, rather than wallowing in my initial reactions. Finding a way to replace shame (it's about me) with understanding (what *is* it about?)

Let me show you what I mean by describing a few possible disappointments and their antidote, enlightenment.

I didn't get the job. I feel fear and rejection. With enlightenment, I can see that I wasn't the best candidate for the job. If I had gotten it, I would have constantly felt insecure. Better to look for something more suited to me where I can excel, or better to educate myself more in the field of my interest, so I can go after that same kind of job but feel more prepared and more secure.

I didn't hear from a guy I recently met. I feel rejected. With enlightenment, I see that he wasn't attracted enough to me for us to have made a go of it. If he'd called me and then withdrawn, I would have been disappointed later, when he and I had more at stake. He didn't reject me! He knew something about himself that told him that I wasn't right for him. And if I wasn't right for him, how could he be right for me? I need a man who adores me, not one who feels ambivalent at best.

I wasn't invited anywhere for Christmas. I feel rejected and lonely. With enlightenment, I see that my friends have their own families and their own life, and it's not about me. The fact may be that I don't have many friends. Why not? Do I want to invest the energy necessary to create new relationships? Is that important to me? Do I care about Christmas anyway?

I wasn't invited to speak at some convention. I feel belittled and invalidated. With enlightenment, I see that it is not I, but only my ego, that's disappointed. The rest of me was thrilled to stay home for the weekend and work on my book. Or maybe what I'm saying isn't very interesting to anyone but me, and I need to face that fact. Or maybe I'm ahead of or behind the times, and that's just life. In any case, my work is for my edification, and it doesn't matter what others think.

Every disappointment brings the possibility of enlightenment, because it disrupts the flow of some expectation and causes me to stop and think. And this brings balm for the soul and opportunity for self-knowledge.

When I am unconscious, I merely react and feel hurt. When I have awareness, I step out of my reactions and see reality. Reality I can deal with. Personalizing everything is the killer.

So does this mean that I'm thrilled to have disappointments? Does this mean I ask the universe to bring them on, so that I can increase my enlightenment?

Are you kidding? But then, I don't have to. Reality provides plenty of opportunities for enlightenment without any help from me.

31

"Slow down to speed up. It's better to get somewhere slowly than nowhere fast."

Why do I try to rush things? Usually because I feel anxious, either because of internal or external causes. But if I'm already anxious, rushing will only make me more so, because we all know that the more anxious we are, the more mistakes we make, which makes us more anxious yet.

Sure, sometimes we need to move swiftly, but rushing is not about the speed of movement; it's about skipping steps, trying to avoid the necessary developmental process.

Let's say I imagine that it's better to be a woman than a little girl. I steal into mom's room and put on her high heeled shoes. Have I gone through the necessary process of growing up? No. And in trying to rush the process of maturation, all I see in the mirror is a little girl who wobbles.

It's clear that we can't rush our process. If I rush a relationship, I might find myself with the wrong woman, a baby and a whole lot of trouble. If I try to rush this book, I might be unclear and lose the opportunity to share with you.

Slow down to speed up applies to our spiritual journey in a major way. If we're rushing to "get" somewhere spiritually, we're defeating ourselves. The only way to speed up our process is to slow down and thoroughly learn each lesson that is presented to us.

This is not easy for me. I want to do everything yesterday and know everything today. And I want to be physically, emotionally and spiritually well right now! It's perfectly normal that I have these thoughts and desires. I believe that spiritual healing will make me happier, so naturally I'm in a hurry. And it will, to a degree. But I can't stress myself trying to get more relaxed, can I?

Rushing our evolution doesn't work. God has already told us that we'd better start liking the process because that's all there is. And he's told us that everything is a transition to the next transition. And we've been told we can't do the right thing for the wrong reason.

So wouldn't this add up to, "Why be in such a darned hurry to arrive at some place of peace and contentment, when you won't stay there; you're just going to start evolving to the next transition anyway? And if your motive for rushing is to avoid discomfort, aren't you doing something for the wrong reason?"

Yes it's true that ultimately there is more peace when we've done a lot of healing. But we can't rush that. We have to do the work. There are no shortcuts. Every part of us needs to come into alignment, every aspect of our consciousness. And every trauma and constellation of fears and negativity needs to be released. How can we rush that?

Evolution. It's just a big job, and if we're smart, we'll take our time and be thorough. If we don't, we just think we're jumping ahead only to find ourselves back where we started.

Our psyches and the universe are conspiring to bring us to wellness, if that's our desire. So slow down to speed up. It's better to get somewhere slowly than nowhere fast.

32

"Love and compassion mean more than spiritual purity."

There's a cute story that goes along with this aphorism, and I'd like to share it with you.

This happened in 1981. I was early in my spiritual growth and was receiving a flow of messages through my newly-discovered inner voice. As a result, I thought I was a pretty significant spiritual being, who was being prepared for some pretty significant spiritual work. Ah yes, spiritual ego.

At the same time, my husband and I were extremely poor. I was working as a temp typist, and he had no income at all.

One day I received a refund check for $50 from Blue Cross. I knew that I didn't deserve the money and that it was a mistake. What to do?

On the one hand, this could have been a way that the universe was channeling desperately needed funds to me. In that case, I should say thank you. On the other, it might be a test of my integrity, in which case I should say no.

Between the honesty I had learned as a child and the belief that my integrity was of utmost importance as a spiritual being, I contacted Blue Cross and tried to return the funds. I spoke to several people, and each one refused. They had no idea how the error had been made, and it would have cost them a fortune to find it.

"Please," they said to me, "keep the money. If we ever find the error, we'll notify you and ask for the money back."

I, however, was still troubled, and I was considering returning the money to them over their objections.

At that time, I lived in Los Angeles and daily took the bus to work. One day as I was waiting for the bus thinking about my dilemma, God spoke to me.

"Are you smiling, Beth?" she asked.

Well, of course not. I was pondering an important spiritual issue. What a ridiculous question.

At that moment, I came out of myself and my self-obsession. I looked around and become aware of my surroundings. There were people standing at the bus stop with me, and I hadn't smiled at one of them. I also realized that I was having no compassion for the poor employees at Blue Cross, who had no idea what to do with the $50, if I returned it to them in order to enhance my virtue.

What a lesson. I'll never forget it. I had been looking for the spiritual test, but I had missed it entirely. I realized then that while I was focusing on my theoretical purity, I had missed the point of spirituality entirely, which was for me to become more loving and open, a person more compassionate with myself and others, including the workers at Blue Cross.

At that point I laughed at myself, decided to forget about returning the money and turned to greet my neighbors. I had indeed passed the test.

33

"Either God is everything, or God is nothing."

We've already discussed the idea that our beliefs are mental constructs, ideas of the mind that we confuse with truths. Nowhere is this more obvious than in our arguments about God. Nevertheless, let me share with you an aphorism from God about God, which says that God is either everything or nothing. It's an idea you may find useful.

Many of us have a sense that our universe has a source, and we call that source God. Past that, we define God in many different ways. In the Judeo-Christian tradition, for example, we see God as all-powerful, all-knowing and everywhere at once. But at the same time, many of us say that God is love but not hate; goodness not evil. Now, obviously there's a problem here. If God is all-powerful and everywhere, then there can't be anything that isn't God.

If God is the source of everything, then God is everything I like and everything I don't like. I can't pick and choose. God is Mother Theresa and Osama bin Laden; God is black, and God is white; even the absence of God is God.

God is often referred to as the light. Ordinary white light, like that from the sun, looks colorless. Yet we know that if it passes through a prism, we can see that it is made up of a band of colors, each of which is made up of different wavelengths.

When it rains, the air is filled with raindrops, which act like a prism, and when we're lucky and the light comes through the drops at a particular angle, we get to see that spectrum. We don't judge that. We love it.

Wouldn't it be wonderful if we could accept that God is the spectrum of the rainbow and not just the colors we choose? Then we wouldn't be busy figuring out which color is God and which isn't, and we wouldn't be stuck with the confusing idea that God is one and within everything, except the things, people and events we don't like.

There are a lot of life experiences that we don't enjoy, and there are parts of ourselves we don't like, but if God is the source, God is the source of it all. To make peace with that is the work of a lifetime. With this aphorism, that work becomes easier. When something happens that upsets me, or if I see a quality in myself that causes me pain, I acknowledge that it is of God, because either God is everything, or God is nothing. I can try to change things I don't like, but I don't separate them from God.

In my view, God is evolving in an evolving universe. So, if I don't like something, I look at it this way: This is happening as a part of evolution. This concept may not be "true," because there is no "truth", but it certainly allows me to be more peaceful and more able to live with reality, as I know it. And it allows me to be more at peace with God.

God is everything, or God is nothing. I have to remember that every time I become distressed or afraid. If I can have that kind of faith, I can relax.

So the next time you're distressed or afraid, try to remember that God is white light filtered through a prism. Then you never have to run away from any aspect of reality, because we need all colors to come together as white, because everything is God.

34

"You can never gain enlightenment at another's expense."

How silly, you might say. Who needs this aphorism? Who would do a thing like that?

Many years ago, I worked in downtown Los Angeles, and I commuted with a friend of mine. I was hot in the pursuit of my spiritual development, and every free moment was devoted to it.

In those days, I couldn't "hear" the inner voice, so I used a pendulum to point out letters that I drew in a circle. It was my homemade ouija board.

One morning, my pendulum was dancing, notifying me that I had a very important message coming. Important message, huh? I looked at the clock and realized that it was time to leave. My friend would be waiting for me, but on the other hand I really wanted to hear what God had to say.

There was a tense moment while I fought with myself. I really wanted to get my message, but it didn't seem fair to make my friend wait. After a brief hesitation, I decided to go. If the message was that important, it would come through when I got home. If it didn't come through, it couldn't have been that important anyway.

Of course, when I got home, there was no message. Or rather, I realized that I had already gotten it. The message was that I couldn't hurt my friend to gain my enlightenment.

Sometimes we become so obsessed with our own spiritual progress, we don't realize that we're trying to gain it at the expense of another.

This aphorism doesn't apply just to spirituality. Don't we do the same thing in other ways? I'm so obsessed with my writing, I neglect the dog. I'm so obsessed with my career, I forget myself and my family. I'm so obsessed with getting ahead, I forget the people I'm trampling to get there.

Nothing can be gained at another's expense. We may gain something of little value in the short run; but we will lose everything of real value in the long run.

35

"Peace always finds those who seek it."

Now what exactly does that mean? Peace always *finds* those who seek it. Does that make sense?

In my struggles to find peace in my heart, there have been times when I have felt no peace at all. I would be striving for understanding and self-control, trying to quiet the turmoil in my mind and aiming for the wisdom to live a more balanced life. But there were times—sometimes even months—when no matter what I did, I was a mess.

One day, when I was beating myself up one more time for not feeling peaceful, God told me that peace would find me. Wow, what a concept!

I didn't really know what it meant, but I knew I could relax. No, I don't mean that I stopped working on myself or stopped trying to develop new ways of acting and reacting. But I do mean that I stopped worrying about the immediate result. Who cared if I was a mess? At some point, all my efforts would bear fruit, and peace would find me.

I don't want to tell you how many years it's taken for me to achieve the level of peace that I have attained, and even this level of peace gets shaken up pretty regularly. But passage of time doesn't matter. It's part of the process.

So where am I now? Along the journey, I've had many highs and lows, moments of joy and weeks of misery, hours of peace and months of anguish. But I can honestly say the tide has turned, and I have fewer moments of anguish and many more hours of peace. Yes, peace has found me.

If you're troubled by the state of your emotions and your mind, remember this aphorism. If you continue to do the work of healing and clearing, if you continue to seek peace and wellbeing, if you continue to do your part, peace will find you.

It found me.

36

"Why worry about God's judgment? You couldn't possibly know what I think anyway."

We are so used to living in the shame/blame universe that we assume that God is judging us, too. Many of us grew up with religious beliefs based on a judgmental God, and our world generally teaches us to find fault and punish. If there's a flood, someone didn't engineer the house right. If there's a rape, the girl invited it, the police didn't prevent it, or the man's parents didn't catch his mental illness when he was a teen.

Of course individuals are responsible and contribute to bad things happening. But it is equally true that our first instinct is to try to find someone to scapegoat, so that we can fix the problem by punishing "them." Then "we" can feel secure that "it" will never happen again and "we" can go back to business as usual. Yeah, the house was engineered wrong, but by blaming "them", we won't have to question the policy of building on hillsides to start with.

Does God judge? No. God is the totality of all being, and, therefore, everything we do, say and think is part of God. If God were to judge us, she would be judging herself.

God's plan is beyond our narrow categories of good and bad, right and wrong; it's about experience and evolution. God is not conceptual, caught in mental constructs of good and evil. And God is not interested in crime or punishment.

It is we, not God, who judge, and for good reason—because we suffer the consequences of everything we do and everything everyone else does. It is natural that we seek to control everyone's behavior, so that we may make life easier, happier and less traumatic for us. But natural or not, judgment, along with its handmaidens of shame and blame, does not contribute to the creation of a more constructive way of living. On the contrary. When we judge someone, we isolate them, as if they were the only bad ones. Oh, he's greedy, or lazy or out of control. Of course, we are, too, but we're so afraid of being judged, we quickly cast the first stone, hoping nobody notices our shortcomings. The isolated person feels afraid, defensive, angry and small, which blocks him from learning and becoming a more constructive person.

Accountability is different from judgment. It requires 1) that we acknowledge the pain our behavior causes and 2) that we make appropriate amends. With accountability, we develop and grow larger. Accountability is necessary, and it must be learned, but we will only do so when we feel the safety of compassion, not the fear of judgment

Life is going to be out of control, but it can be improved, not by judging and punishing one another, but by helping each other to become happier and more balanced. Happy and balanced people tend to be less destructive. So while we may have to stop one another from committing destructive acts, we need to focus on letting go of our tendency to judge and replacing that approach with a commitment to help.

So let's stop worrying about God's judgments or using God's name to control ourselves or others. Let it be enough that we know there's a better way to live and that we are willing to work for it.

37

"Don't be impatient for enlightenment. Patience is as much a part of enlightenment as the lesson you are impatient to learn."

Ooh, that hurt. I have always been impatient. When I was little, I wanted to be an adult. When I'm reading a book, I want to know what happens. So much for life is a journey.

As I mentioned in relation to an earlier aphorism, we're impatient because we're uncomfortable where we are, and we want to end our discomfort. The only way we think we can end our discomfort is to end the experience. And we're impatient to do it. But to get comfortable, we need to change ourselves, and for that we need patience.

So, what's so great about patience, and what's the difference between that and passivity? Let's start with passivity. Passivity means I have given up on myself and think I have no power. Let's say a puppy tries ten times to jump on the bed. If he becomes discouraged, he won't try again, because he won't want to re-experience the pain of failure. But he has motivation, and he keeps trying. On the other hand, if he's chewing up our favorite furniture, we create an unpleasant experience and he stops. Why doesn't he get passive about jumping on the bed but does, hopefully, stop chewing shoes? Because the negative experience of falling off the bed is felt by him as emotionally neutral, whereas chewing the furniture is accompanied by our disapproval.

Are we different? If we're passive, perhaps we have given up, not just because we've failed a few times, but because we got the message that we shouldn't do something. Maybe we weren't encouraged to continue, or were even shamed for trying. Patience is the opposite of passivity; it's about perseverance over time and despite failures. It is what it takes to keep trying until we get it right.

Patience is part of enlightenment, because it's about understanding the process of development. It requires us to look deeply into the areas where we want to move forward and to realize what is required for us to do so. For our puppy, for example, jumping requires the development of strength and coordination, which only time and exercise provide.

Patience is part of enlightenment also, because it requires us to understand our connection to the universe, that there may be factors outside ourselves, as well as within us, that need to be in place in order for us to move forward. I could be the greatest teacher, for example, but if there are no students, I have to be patient until the kids are ready for school.

And, finally, patience is part of enlightenment, because we learn that even those factors in ourselves that need to change may not change until the universe supports that development. I may be impatient to heal, for example, but I need to wait until the universe provides a healer who understands my condition or until I can learn to heal myself.

We may dislike our emotional state or living conditions, but sometimes we need to endure. Endurance keeps us going, while we patiently, yet actively work toward the developments that will allow us to change.

38

"Don't let the paucity of your vision limit the expanse of your soul."

First, for those of you who aren't sure what this means, paucity means poverty or lack. So the aphorism says that we shouldn't be limited by the vision we already have, because our vision is in itself limited.

I love this aphorism because it lifts the soul.

We have no idea who we are and who we could be, and that's the fun of it. But it would be so much better if all of us carried this awareness.

God communicated this aphorism when I was just beginning my work as an intuitive counselor. At that time I had a vision of who I was and what I might achieve. I was full of ego and short on experience! I thought that I would become famous, attract lots of clients, and create an organization that supported the intuitive work I was then doing.

None of the above happened, and at times I have felt pretty low. Yet now, more than twenty years later, both my work and I have grown into something way more than I could ever have envisioned. My path has been full of the most unexpected twists and turns, and the outcome is different and greater than I could have imagined.

Our finite minds only know what we've experienced or can see, and so even our dreams are based on what we know. The most wild stirrings of the imagination are still based on concepts and images we've garnered from life. A walk on the moon, travels in space, all dreamed of in the past and accomplished. Yet the physics of today has opened new vistas and new amazement.

Before we knew about DNA, we could not have imagined gene therapy. Before we had the computer, we couldn't have imagined recording orchestral music on a keyboard in our own livingroom.

Yes, for all of us there is an unknown, a place to which the future calls us in the process of becoming. We can't imagine it, because imagining uses the mind that is limited, but some of us may be able to sense it, because that sense relies on a connection to the infinite.

You may think you know where you and your life are going, but most of us have found that experience leads us in ways very different from our expectations. If you embrace the unexpected path, if you keep growing, instead of giving up through the many disappointments and turns you encounter, you may find yourself a deeper and more wonderful person than you could have imagined.

Let your life and the universe take you into the unknown. Don't let the paucity of your vision limit the expanse of your soul.

39

"Love is like a volleyball game. You must connect and release."

I was teaching a class once, and God suggested an experiment. We started by envisioning a volleyball that represented love, and then we bounced it around the circle.

As in volleyball, the trick was to connect to the ball and release it to the person of our choice, because if we didn't pass it on immediately, the ball would fall, and the game would come to an end.

As we sent the love to one another, we would say that we were now passing the love to John, or Terry, or Helen or whoever was next, so that the next person would be prepared to pass the ball again.

The most amazing thing happened during the game. As each of us passed the ball to the next, we all started to feel more loved. It didn't matter to whom we passed the ball, we all felt the energy. Yes, I guess we really are one.

In love, as in life, we can't hang on to anything. We need to connect and release to keep the flow of energy that nurtures us all. If someone shows us love at any given moment, we can accept it only if we can release it. If we don't release the love, this is what will happen. Instead of feeling the love itself, we'll be feeling the fear of losing it.

Whenever we focus on something's loss, we already lose it, because our attention is on the fear of its loss, rather than the experience of the thing itself.

I was married to a man who was sober from alcoholism for eleven years. Eventually, he went out and drank again. But if I had focused on my fear of losing him to the bottle, I would have lost those wonderful years. Fortunately in that case, I focused on the love and not the fear of losing it.

Love is not a possession. It's an experience. And like life itself, love must be released in order to be appreciated.

40

"It is no more noble to abuse yourself than it is to abuse others."

Some of us think that sacrificing ourselves is a virtue. It's not. We are all one, and if we abuse ourselves, we're actually abusing us all.

Let's think for a minute in practical terms. I'm the hardworking dad who's been stressing himself out to support his family. I've eaten badly and neglected my health. Now my diabetes is out of control, and I lose my foot. Up to this point, I didn't have the heart to ask my kids to get odd jobs to help support the family. Now everyone has to take care of me. Oops.

I am the sacrificing mom, who hasn't had a moment's rest in days. I won't ask for help, because I don't want to impose on others. When the baby has thrown the peas on the floor for the fifth time, I'm ready to explode. Instead, I control myself and bend down again. I don't have the heart to even gently discipline the baby. But doesn't that baby feel my anger? Doesn't it actually get stressed out by my feelings and probably throw the peas again, just out of anxiety?

I'm the diligent worker who has come into the office seven days a week, six weeks in a row. I don't feel good about saying no to my boss and asking her to get extra help. By the end of the third week, I'm getting bleary-eyed, and by the end of the sixth, I don't even know what mistakes I'm making. My work has gone downhill, and I'm so exhausted, I need a long break. Who has benefited from this?

We abuse ourselves in numerous other ways, such as drinking, overeating, taking drugs, exhausting ourselves to help others, and criticizing ourselves. When we drink or overeat, we hurt everyone by destroying our health and by losing our productivity. When we take drugs, we endanger others at work and on the road. We may even lose our functioning altogether and need to be cared for. When we exhaust ourselves to help others, we end up sick, which causes us to drain everyone else. And when we criticize ourselves endlessly, we are so tense that we snap off other people's heads.

There is nothing noble about self-abuse. In fact self-abuse is irresponsible. It denies the responsibility we have to ourselves and to God, our source, to care for the being that we are. And it denies our responsibility to everyone else, who ultimately has to pick up the pieces.

On a spiritual plane, we are all one, and the abuse of one is the abuse of all. And it's obvious from the above we don't have to look far to see how this plays out in daily life.

So the next time you want to sacrifice yourself, ask yourself the motive. Are you trying to win love, impress or look noble? Then have a good laugh, and remember that it's no more noble to abuse yourself than it is to abuse others.

41

"Shit happens. Turn it into fertilizer."

I like this idea, and it keeps me going.

I don't always like God, and I rarely like what I see in the world. People hurt one another; accidents happen; and sweet people get a raw deal.

My own life has hardly been a bowl of cherries, and I think lots of "unfair" things have happened to me and everybody else.

But what should I do?

Well, I could complain, and I do. But ultimately that gets old. I'm so bored with my own complaining, I could croak. And, guess what? You get bored with my complaining, too.

If I want to feel good, I have to change my state. So I've developed a technique that works well for me. I rationalize everything that happens and give it a positive interpretation. Or, if I can't find a positive interpretation, I still find a way to make it support my growth.

Do I always believe in these rationalizations? No. But I convince myself that I do, and boy do I feel better! And more important, can I always find a way to have these experiences support my growth? Absolutely.

One day years ago, I took a weekend vacation in a mountain community in Southern California. On the way up the mountain, I got a message from God that I was going to the mountain to open my heart. Sounds cool, right?

While I was there, I decided to look at some property, which is something I really enjoy doing. As the realtor was showing me a house, I twisted my ankle walking down some uneven steps. It was a terrible ankle twisting, and I ended up crippled for months. In the midst of experiencing this excruciating fall, I said to myself, "Wow, this must be part of the opening of my heart." Sounds ridiculous, doesn't it?

By good fortune, I was staying overnight at a motel with a friend, who kindly took care of me. And the realtor, whom I just met, offered to drive my car down the mountain the next week and return it to me. Because of my poor health, I was so impacted by the fall I had to get a roommate. And many other results occurred. All of these had to do with opening my heart—or so I told myself.

I could tell you about much more traumatic life experiences that I've rationalized or turned into the fertilizer of my spiritual growth. You may laugh and call me nuts, but one thing I can tell you for sure: I am a better person for it.

I do not rationalize what happens to other people. I cannot tell someone that it was for their own good to have been burned by their parents as a child. But I can always help them find something in the experience from which they can grow.

I don't always agree with the teachings that everything happens for our own good or that you're never given more to bear than you can. I have seen too many people crushed by their experiences and blocked by circumstances that stop their growth. But I do know one thing for sure, which is that if you have the inner capacity and enough support to turn shit into fertilizer, do it. The growth you fertilize is your own, and you will be a happier person for it.

42

"Fear and faith are not opposites. If you didn't have fear, you wouldn't need faith."

During my spiritual journey, I have learned a lot about fear and how to handle it. One of the teachings I've heard that isn't necessarily true for me is: "When you have faith, you don't have fear."

Early on, God told me the opposite: that if you didn't have fear, you wouldn't need faith, and this works for me.

I understand on a more sophisticated level now that fear is a natural and important aspect of our emotional makeup. If we didn't have it, we'd die.

If we didn't fear getting burned, we'd leap into fires. If we didn't fear death, we'd all drive with our eyes shut. And if we didn't fear one another's violence, we'd probably get even nastier than we do when we get into arguments.

It isn't fear itself, but fear out of balance that is our problem. My favorite example is this: Let's say you're walking over the railroad tracks, and the train is coming. If you have no fear, you'll stand there and get run over. If you have too much fear, you'll freeze and get run over. But if you have just the right amount of fear, you'll get your ass in gear and get off the tracks.

In life, fear is natural and useful, but when we've been traumatized, we can become overwhelmed by fear and then we become paralyzed, unable to be free and creative in our responses. That's when we have to build up our faith.

When I think of faith, I really mean faith in myself and in my emotional wellness. When scary things face me, I tell myself that everything is going to be all right, meaning that whatever happens, I will be able to cope.

I have no illusions. I know that painful and difficult experiences await me on a daily basis, but I also know that if I don't know how to handle problems, I have the inner resources to seek out help and figure it out.

I have another kind of faith, too, faith in my connection to the infinite, faith in my connection to God. To me, that means that no matter what happens to me, I will find a way to hang on to my essence, my inner self, so that it and I will continue to grow in love and wisdom, rather than give in to defeat and despair.

Yes, I have fear, but I also have faith.

It's doesn't get better than that.

43

"A block is just a directional signal."

I like to be in charge, don't you? That means, I decide what I want to do and what I want the outcome to be. How often does any of this work out?

Before I became a full-time intuitive counselor, I had many jobs. One of them was as the assistant to the vice president of a market research company. I knew nothing about market research; nor was I particularly interested in it. But it paid the bills, and that was my aim.

After working with the vice president for a year, I had risen in the firm. He had me doing special projects and research, and I really enjoyed it. He also gave me a big raise.

One day, my boss up and quit, and under the new regime, the work changed. Instead of those special projects, I had to do the regular market research, analyzing data and crunching numbers. I had absolutely no background, education or affinity for this, and I flopped miserably.

Did I try to fit myself into the mold! It was pathetic.

Finally the new vice president called me in and told me they were offering me two choices: Either they would cut my salary, or I should quit.

Of course, I was outraged and humiliated and wanted to quit. But I was scared of being without a paycheck during a time when jobs were scarce.

I went home and meditated on what to do. In the meditation, I saw myself walking through the jungle. I came to a fork in the road, where there was a sign that said "One way."

Great. One way. Which way?

Upon further reflection, I understood the message. I was totally unsuited to the work that I was trying to force myself to do, and the boss was perfectly right to cut my pay. There was really only one appropriate response. Why torment myself or those good people who were trying compassionately to keep me in a job? We would all be better off if I left and they could hire a person more suited to the work.

What at first looked like a block in my life, the threat to my income, was really a directional signal to leave a profession ill suited to me. I accepted the message, resigned and was out on the street.

Fascinating things happen in life, don't they? Within a week, I had a temporary job that ended up lasting two years. I became the communications coordinator of an international school, where I met many fascinating people and utilized my skills. I didn't leave that job until it was time for me to assume my intuitive counseling work fulltime.

Every day I find myself blocked. I'm too sick to write, my volunteer administrator quits, the IRS sends us a letter telling us we're not in compliance, a client cancels, and I have no clue as to what to do. Instead of panicking, I've learned to relax, clear my feelings, regroup and change gears.

Every block is a sign that says, "One way." Sometimes that one way sign means wait; sometimes it means go left, go right or go over.

The more I relax and allow the block to guide me, the less frustrated and angry I am, and the more I can enjoy the way life is.

44

"Don't strive. Stretch."

What's the difference between stretching and striving? Let me explain.

To strive is to have an external goal that you're trying to reach. You are striving to achieve something, create something, be something, accomplish something. To stretch is to start with who and what you are and extend yourself from there.

Is this an important difference? You bet it is. If I'm striving to lose twenty pounds, then a certain weight is my goal. If I were stretching myself, I would try to improve my eating habits and see where my body's weight wants to land.

Striving toward an external goal often leads us to self-abuse. I may be trying to force myself into a size 5, even though my bone structure would be more comfortably accommodated by a size 11. In this case, I'm choosing a goal that is actually unnatural and unhealthy for me. If I get angry at myself for failing to reach this unnatural goal, then I've added emotional abuse to the abuse of my body.

It's no different when our goal relates to career. If I strive to be a graphic artist when I don't have the talent, I'm going to torture myself and blame everyone else.

Why would I take on a goal that is so unsuitable? Because I have some idea in my head that accomplishing that goal will give me value in my own eyes, as well as in the eyes of other people.

When I stretch, I start with what is and extend myself. Take our example of the graphic artist: If I've got a flair for graphic design, I can stretch and try to get hired into an art department. If I've got the talent, that stretch will land me a job from which I can stretch again. If I don't have the talent, the stretch will be to let myself go another way. Or, if I can be hired into a low-level job but can't advance, the stretch may be for me to stay at that level and be satisfied.

If I'm striving to be an artist because that's what my parents would like me to be or because of the prestige I think I will gain, I'm not being true to myself. I'm not valuing my own nature and gifts. Instead, I'm trying to fill a role, rather than stretching to fulfill myself.

Stretching and striving have a lot to do with the way we grow spiritually. If I'm striving to be an enlightened being, I will make myself nuts. Here's an example. One day I was asking God about whether or not it was okay to kill a moth. I hated the idea of killing, but I honestly didn't want the moth flying in my mouth or eating my clothes.

God answered me perfectly. "If the day comes when you feel ready to stop killing moths, you will. Until that time, don't worry about it."

Sometimes we have to stretch out of our comfort zone, and that's part of our growth. We need to care for an elderly relative, when we don't think we can. We have to develop understanding and patience with our children, when we can't imagine how. As long as we are extending our capacities, rather than aiming for some external goal, such as *looking* like the devoted son or the perfect mom, we're stretching ourselves, and it's a good experience.

Somewhere we've gotten the idea that we should create goals and try to achieve them. The only goal that's realistic is to stretch in the direction we want every day and see where that takes us. The results don't matter. After all, it's only the stretch that counts anyway.

45

"A dream is something to work toward. A fantasy is something you can never achieve."

The differences between a dream and a fantasy: One gives you momentum, and the other keeps you paralyzed. One makes you feel positive about yourself, and the other is a source of shame.

If I am paraplegic, I may fantasize about running a marathon. At the end of the fantasy, I'm still in the wheelchair, and I'm feeling frustration and despair. But if I am that same paraplegic, I may dream of participating in the Special Olympics for folks in wheelchairs. I can move on that dream and see how I can realize it.

If I fantasize about being a 5'10", smooth-skinned beauty, with long blond silky hair, I'm only denying the beauty of the petite wrinkled woman in the mirror, the one whose hair has a mind of its own. And I can't make it happen anyway. But if I dream of loving myself as I am, I have a path to walk; it's the path of self-love. That I can work for.

If you sit in front of the computer, fantasizing in front of pornographic photos, you're not working toward a relationship you can have. If you dream of developing your relationship with the woman in the kitchen, you can work toward that dream or let the relationship go.

Dreams keep us going. Fantasies keep us stuck. Dreams give us direction. Fantasies send us nowhere.

It's not always easy to tell the difference between a dream and a fantasy, and sometimes we have to give something a try to find out.

If I dream of improving my relationship with you, but you don't want to stay in the marriage, then I'm harboring a fantasy. But I won't find that out until I come to you with my hopes and ask you to join me on the journey.

If you're a handyman who would like to be a physicist but you've never finished high school, ask yourself if you have the motivation to confront all the requirements to get you where you want to go. If you're not willing to do the work, you're in fantasy. If, on the other hand, your dream is to build a handyman business of integrity, where you support yourself and help others, and you're willing to do the work, you've got a dream.

In some ways it's easier to stick with fantasy, rather than allow yourself dreams. When you're in fantasy, you probably know it and know also that there is nothing you can really do, so you can justify giving up, eating some popcorn and watching TV. In other words, you can justify doing nothing and not stretching at all. If we stay stuck in fantasy, there's no space for our dreams and with no dreams, we have no motivation, no hope and nowhere to go.

A fantasy can transform into a dream. For example, I would like to see a more compassionate, mutually-supportive world. I can't make that happen, and it could be a fantasy. But what if I want to help co-create such a world? That's a dream I can work toward every day.

Not all our dreams come true, of course. The dream calls us, we set out on the course, and then we discover what life has in store. After all, the dream is something to work toward, not to achieve.

46

"Nobody has too much power.
They don't have enough."

This message is counter-intuitive. We look at people who wield power, and we think they have too much, not too little. We intuitively feel we should bring them down a peg.

Bullies in the schoolyard, imperious politicians, greedy bosses, abusive parents, the punk with the gun, these people can make our lives miserable. But do they have too much power? Are they in fact acting out of a sense of power, or out of a sense of powerlessness?

Truly powerful people don't need to make themselves feel good by making you feel bad. They don't need to make themselves big by making you small. They don't need to make themselves happy by making you miserable.

The truth is that people who abuse power feel powerless, or they wouldn't feel the need to abuse.

The bully in the schoolyard is probably being beaten by his dad or is afraid of being dominated by other kids. The political leader who irresponsibly sends us to war knows he has blood on his hands, and the nightmare of his culpability makes him feel scared. He's now even more likely to pretend to us and himself that his choices were just. Employers who are greedy are scared people, grabbing for themselves because of their insecurities. They feel afraid of their employees' judgment and act like it's their employees who are greedy. Abusive parents can see the fear in the eyes of their children, but they have no power over their own violence. They know they are out of control, so they wait until they're drunk, pretend their abuse is less than it is or justify their behavior. And the punk with the gun is scared of being exposed as the impotent kid he knows he is.

The only true power is the power we have over ourselves. Those who can regulate their reactions and behavior don't need to abuse, exploit or hide their mistakes. They consult, admit fault, and make choices based on the highest good of all, rather than the highest benefit to their egos. And they support others to be powerful as well, because others' power is no threat to theirs.

When we look at people who damage others through their abuse of power, we are seeing powerless people, people who feel powerless on the inside and who are powerless over themselves. The most useful action we can take is to send their way whatever help we can offer, so they may achieve greater self-love and wellbeing, so that they will become truly powerful on the inside and not need to be powerful on the outside.

It's not easy to transcend our contempt toward those who we believe abuse power; nor is it easy to support them spiritually when they're hurting us or others. And there are certainly times when we need to use whatever force is necessary to stop their actions. But stopping their actions can only be the beginning. If we don't support these souls to gain their own sense of worth, restraining them will only make them feel more powerless, which will only increase their motivation to act out again.

So, remember, when you think about people whose power you resent, "Nobody has too much power. They don't have enough." Let's see how we can help empower one another.

47

"Everyone wakes up in the morning with the same need: to feel loved and validated."

After the September 11th attack on the World Trade Center, I spoke to a group of people about a spiritual approach to the experience. I challenged the listeners to consider the question: Why? Why had the terrorists attacked us? What had driven them to these desperate acts?

The response to my questions was amazing to me. In the minds of the audience, Muslims were not like "us." They were different. We didn't have to understand them, because they were just demons. Wow, that really got us off the hook, didn't it?

I connected to God, and these words came out: "We are all humans, with the same fundamental needs. Although the things we do to gain that love and validation may vary, we all wake up in the morning with the same desire to feel loved and validated. In some places, validation may come from having the most cattle; in some it may come from having the most wives; in some it may come from making the most money. But the motivation is the same."

To my astonishment, the audience disagreed.

Muslims, I was told, were fanatic (genetically?) And they were out to get us. No reason. Just because. When I pointed out that the West had colonized their lands and still tried to control them through military, political or economic means, the audience looked blank. When I pointed out that throughout our history, the United States has assumed the right to install friendly regimes all over the world, the audience wouldn't listen. And when I reminded them of the Christian missionaries, the audience looked aghast. Evidently, in their minds, only Muslims try to force other people to live their way. My listeners refused to see how we do and have done the same things. They refused to learn our own history.

How will we solve the world's problems, if we refuse to see one another's humanity? How will we make peace, if we don't see ourselves clearly? How will we understand one another, if we don't see that we are essentially the same?

Does this sound far-fetched and abstract? What about our experience in our homes? If I look at my husband and refuse to understand his motives, I am making him a nonhuman. And he may do the same to me. At that point, the possibility of reconciliation is dead. Similarly, we'll never make peace or progress if we deny the humanity of the boss, members of the opposition, people of another race, or anybody we disagree with. Once we've denied someone's humanity, we've cut off the ability to understand one another, which is the best chance we have to achieve peace.

Everyone has the same need for love and validation. My husband may neglect me because he's busy trying to make the money to impress his father who died 20 years ago. He's still seeking his dad's love. I may be angry, because I feel neglected, because I'm seeking his. Our behaviors are different, but our motives are the same. We're both seeking love and validation, and we're both suffering from the lack.

The sooner we see our oneness, the sooner we will ask the question, why? And the sooner we will understand and be able to co-create the conditions under which we can all receive the love and validation we so profoundly need.

48

"The first step toward healing is compassion for yourself. The second is compassion for others."

Why is this true? Because compassion for ourselves is the key to self-honesty, and without self-honesty there is no healing.

Many of us have been shamed as part of the experience of learning. You made a mistake. That meant you were stupid or lazy or just not paying attention. You got a B; why not an A? You didn't hit the ball; you "lost" the game for us all. Your hair looks a mess; I don't want to be seen with you. You hit the dog; you're a bad boy. You're pregnant? You're a slut.

Shame is so ingrained in our psyches, we're reluctant to self-examine. None of us wants to experience shame; so few of us look deeply into our own motivations.

The antidote to shame is compassion. Why am I this way? Why do I feel this way? Why did I do that?

Just asking the question liberates our psyche. We're out of defense mode and into inquiry. If we're honest, we'll start seeing clues. If we can't find the answers ourselves, we can seek therapy or other people's wisdom.

Some of our reactions have to do with our early history. When you called off our date, I got angry because of my insecurities. Why did I feel insecure? My mom died when I was two, and I've never felt secure since. I know this is my issue, and I need to deal with it.

Some of our reactions have to do with our current situation. When you called off our date, I got angry because of my insecurities. Why? You've never told me you love me, and you refuse to maintain any kind of commitment. I'm insecure, because you're not offering me any security.

Once we seek to understand rather than to justify our behavior, we've become our own best friend. We can say, yes, I understand why I did this. We are the ally we never had, who can help us forgive ourselves and move on.

Compassion for ourselves opens the door to compassion for others. When we are in shame, we want to blame someone else to relieve our pain. We are too defensive to want to understand the other person's actions and motives.

With compassion, we feel less pain, we're no longer defensive, and we can look and listen. You broke off our date because you were feeling smothered and didn't know what else to do. Okay, I was pressuring you for an immediate commitment, when we haven't known each other long. Yes, I can understand how you would feel pressured. If I were you, I would probably have had the same reaction. It's just because of my insecurities that I feel such a need to pin you down. We're both insecure. What can we do about it?

Compassion doesn't automatically solve all problems or mend all relationships, but it's the doorway to awareness, and without that, healing isn't possible.

So the next time you cause someone else pain, or the next time you find yourself anxious or angry, or the next time you fail to fulfill a commitment, ask yourself why, and do it with compassion. Whatever you have done or felt, with enough exploration you will discover there's a reason. Nope, you're not a bad person; you're just a person with fears and pains that have yet to be resolved. I understand. I am, too.

49

"Self-judgment is not self-honesty."

Just as we think that self-sacrifice is noble, we think self-judgment is self-honesty. It's not. Self-honesty is an act of self-love aimed at strengthening and improving ourselves. Self-judgment is an act of self-hatred, which leaves us anxious, defensive and afraid to fail.

Self-judgment is not an objective evaluation; it has an agenda. The agenda could be to gain favor in God's eyes. If I grovel in front of God, maybe she will give me a break. Or the agenda could be the unconscious need to agree with a parent who was very critical of us. Mom said I was a lazy bum, and so I must be. Or it could simply be the teaching and learning style we learned as a child.

Let's look at some of the ways we experience learning as children. Theoretically a parent or teacher has our interests at heart. But being human, they may have their own agenda. Suppose mom wants to prove she's a better mom than her mother was. Then your mistakes become a threat to her self-esteem, and she gets angry. Or suppose mom is insecure and competitive, and actually wants you to never surpass her. Or suppose she's upset with herself that she never went to college, and she wants to achieve through you.

When a parent or any other teacher has an agenda, she won't be able to clearly see what is best for you; she's too absorbed in what she needs you to be. And when you fail to live up to her requirements of you, you're bad, because you've disappointed *her*. Her disappointment is then expressed as disapproval of you. She has become your critic, rather than your teacher.

When I become my own inner critic, I am doing the same thing to myself. I am not looking at myself objectively and seeing my strengths, weaknesses and capacities to grow; I am unloading onto myself the emotions of disapproval and disappointment. I am not supporting myself to learn; I am blocking my learning by being the critic, the person whose expectations I need to fulfill, regardless of who I am, what I feel and what I can really do.

We all need self-honesty and encouragement. Sometimes that encouragement takes the form of a hug, and sometimes it takes the form of a kick in the butt. But to be encouragement, it must be motivated by love, and it must be tempered with a sense of reality about our capabilities.

We need to give that to ourselves. If I fail at something, I feel the disappointment of the failure. If I continue to love myself, I can see whether my expectations were realistic and try to improve. If I cut off my self-love and replace it with disapproval, I feel shame and self-abandonment. From that place, I become tense and afraid, which in fact makes it way harder for me to learn!

When I am my worst critic, slowly but surely, I become afraid of myself. Ultimately I will become a machine struggling to satisfy my inner critic at the expense of all my other needs, and I will do the same to others. Or I will become passive, with the fear of my inner critic killing my incentive, creativity and willingness to take chances.

If I am to help myself learn, I have to be my own teacher, who loves and encourages me to stretch to my potential. If I find an inner critic mixed in with that teacher, I need to replace that critic with a friend.

50

"If you keep looking to others for your validation, you will forever be their slave."

Yes, but I want him to love me. Yes, but I want her to respect me. Yes, but they've been mean to me.

Who said it wasn't more pleasant to be appreciated than discounted? To be praised than slandered? To be loved than ignored?

I'm with you. I would prefer all the goodies. But I don't want to be dependent on anyone for them.

The problem isn't my need for love; it's my dependence on you to get it; it's the feeling that I'll die if I don't have it. If you're my client and I'm dependent on you for validation, how scary it would be to tell you something that might make you so mad, you'd get angry, cut off my validation and maybe even stop seeing me. If you're my child and I'm dependent on you for love, how could I discipline you, even for your own good? If you're my colleague and I'm dependent on you for respect, what would I do if I came up with a counseling process that you think is for the birds?

If I get fixated on you for my validation or love, I can lose my freedom and then blame you, as in, I couldn't tell my client, my child, my colleague what I thought, because they would have rejected me. It's their fault.

Many times couples have come to me, each with the agenda that I make the other one love, validate and appreciate them. And they're angry at me if I don't.

If you are my clients, of course, part of my job is to see what's getting in the way of you giving one another love, validation and appreciation. But, more important, it's my job to help each one of you learn to live without it.

Even if I could "fix" your partner the way you want me to, you'd be happy in the moment, but you'd never be free. You'd still be dependent on the way they treat you to feel good, and your wellbeing would yo-yo with their moods and attentions. But if I help you overcome your emotional overdependence on them, I'll help you be free for the rest of your life.

You choose.

51

"When you're trying to get away from a person or a situation, it's really yourself you're trying to escape."

No, I don't mean that you should never leave a relationship, a job or an abusive situation. Of course at times leaving is the healthiest thing to do. But more painful than the situation itself is the way we feel about ourselves *in* it.

If you are belittling me, I feel anguish, not just because of your meanness, but because of the way I feel about myself when I'm with you. Perhaps I buy into what you're saying. Yes, I really am a stupid bitch. Or perhaps I am enraged with myself for still being in the relationship and letting myself be abused. Or perhaps I feel stupid, because I knew I shouldn't have gotten involved with you in the first place, because you're just like my ex-husband, and how could I have made that same mistake again?

Feeling stupid is a big one, a big source of shame about ourselves. If you remain afraid of commitment after two years together, and I'm still with you, yelling and moaning, I feel like an idiot. I knew when I met you that you were 43 years old and had never been married. What was I thinking? Or if you're still drinking, gambling, having affairs, or watching pornography after all our heart-to-heart conversations, I feel shame for having believed you every time you promised to stop.

When I feel stupid or like I've let myself down, I get angry at myself, and naturally, in order to deflect that awful self-judgment, I have to get angry at you instead. "You son of a bitch, I knew I shouldn't have trusted you. How could you have done this to me?"

Of course the other person hasn't really done anything to *you*. They've just done what they do. But we, in our self-centered way, interpret everything as being about us. And our prize for this wrong way of thinking is that we get to feel not only the pain of their behavior, but the pain of our judgment of ourselves.

When we feel stupid and stand in judgment of ourselves, it's hard to muster the self-esteem to leave a bad situation. If I'm this stupid, weak or bad, how can I leave the job, the girlfriend, the whatever, and go out on my own? So we become more and more stuck. Yet at the same time the pain of our self-judgment makes us want to flee the relationship immediately. We can't stand for another moment the feeling that we are that stupid, gullible and impotent, and we're desperate to leave the person or situation around whom we feel so bad about ourselves. This conflict—between our fear of leaving and our desperate need to get away from the way we feel about ourselves in the situation—leaves us exhausted and confused. From this place we can have no clarity and no peace of mind.

Whether it's a painful job, relationship or situation, let's take a break from recounting over and over how bad he/she/it is, and let's take a look at how we feel about ourselves in it. If we can find compassion for ourselves, we will understand the pain, fear or hope that has motivated us to stay. We can reclaim our self-love and give ourselves a hug. We will then be able to repair our self-esteem, whether or not we leave the situation. Now that's freedom.

52

"Never compare yourself to where you're going; compare yourself to where you've been."

I have many more of God's little aphorisms to share with you, but God has chosen this adage to close. It's another favorite of mine, because I need it every day. Whether you're using this book or some other means of self-awareness and growth, beware the tendency to judge your progress.

As I've mentioned before, I have had major health problems all my life. I have finally found a healer who is helping me, and I'm currently in the process of getting well. But the process is very long and up and down.

Some days I seem way better; other times I seem to have regressed. And never am I where I want to be. I joke that if I have a hundred and forty symptoms and three get better, it's hard to notice. But the truth is that that's the way most of us heal, and that's the way I'm healing. A step at a time.

When I look at where I've been, I'm impressed with my progress. When I look at where I want to be, I feel discouraged. It was because of that negativity that God recently advised me to always compare myself to where I've been, not to where I'm going.

This aphorism has helped me not only with my physical healing, but with my mental/emotional and spiritual growth as well. And it is helping me be more supportive to others, too.

When I see a client struggling, I feel responsible for their pain. I'm not doing a good enough job. I'm torn between blaming them and blaming myself. Of course neither is productive, though both are natural.

But if I step out of that shame/blame cycle and look realistically, I see that the client has made progress, just not at the pace I've decided would be good for them! And definitely not at the pace that would make me look like a hero in my own mind!

The same could be said of friends, roommates, any loved ones. While I'm impatient for them to accomplish all the changes I think they should make, I'm not appreciating and sufficiently validating the changes they have made.

You may have noticed that this volume of aphorisms has focused a lot on compassion for ourselves, getting out of judgment and becoming our best friend. These fundamental teachings are crucial for our journey, and this is where we start. If God's little aphorisms are to be of any help to us, we must learn how to use them. If we use them to support us, great. If we use them to judge ourselves, they're worse than useless. And only if we use them wisely can we learn more.

The Baal Shem Tov, an 18th century Jewish mystic, once said, "I came to help, not to judge." Obviously judging and helping are not the same.

We need to use these aphorisms to help ourselves, not to judge, and this aphorism helps us do that.

As a counselor, teacher and friend, I would like to help more and judge less. Do I always manage to do that? Of course not. Do I do it more than I used to? Absolutely.

So, compared to where I've been, I'm doing great, and so are you, and that's good enough for me.

I love you, and God bless.

About the Author

Beth Green is an intuitive counselor, spiritual teacher, author, composer and speaker. She's also the spiritual director of The Stream, a nonprofit organization dedicated to supporting everyone to reach their potential.

Beth has written several other books, including *The Autobiography of Mary Magdalene*, and *Sacred Union: The Healing of God*. Also a musician, Beth composed and performed the music for two New Age/Classical CDs, *The Gift of Peace* and *A Soul's Journey through Darkness & Light*. In addition, she has produced a number of spoken audiotapes.

Beth has also developed The Living with Reality program, which teaches us to think and feel differently, so we can become more free, more relaxed and more authentically ourselves. The program has three components: 1) her book, *Living with Reality: Nine Platforms for Becoming Ourselves*; 2) donation-based mutual support meetings; 3) a powerful series of workshops that combine spiritual teaching, emotional healing and energetic clearing. This program is sponsored by The Stream.

For information about Beth's counseling, ongoing groups and workshops, go to The Stream website, www.thestream.org. There you will also find ordering information for all her books, tapes and music.

God's Little Aphorisms is also available directly from iUniverse, as well as online distributors, such as Amazon.com and barnesandnoble.com.

Beth Green was born in New York City, where she started her life as a social activist. In 1980, while living in California, she had a dramatic spiritual/psychic awakening, which changed her life. At that time, she became an intuitive counselor and spiritual teacher. She currently offers intuitive counseling, in person and via the phone, ongoing groups and workshops. She is also available as a teacher, speaker and media guest. Beth lives in Southern California with her dog, Sasha.

0-595-34522-0

www.ingramcontent.com/pod-product-compliance
Lightning Source LLC
Chambersburg PA
CBHW020307290526
45784CB00003B/1394